Pro-Verb Ponderings

Pro-Verb Ponderings

31 Ruminations on Positive Action

by

RODNEY BOYD

WordCrafts

Pro-Verb Ponderings
  31 Ruminations on Positive Action
Copyright © 2014
Rodney Boyd

Cover photography & design by David Warren

All rights reserved. No part of this book may be reproduced, stored in a retrieval system, or transmitted in any form or by any means – electronic, mechanical, photocopy, recording, or otherwise – without the prior written permission of the publisher. The only exception is brief quotations for review purposes.

Unless otherwise noted, all scripture quotations are taken from the New American Standard Bible®, Copyright © 1960, 1962, 1963, 1968, 1971, 1972, 1973, 1975, 1977, 1995 by The Lockman Foundation. Used by permission. (www.Lockman.org)

References to "Strong's" refer to *Strong's Exhaustive Concordance of the Bible*, public domain.

Published by WordCrafts Press
Tullahoma, TN 37388
www.wordcrafts.net

DEDICATION

I dedicate these Positive Ponderings to my Pro-Verbs 31 Wife, Brenda. From the beginning of our relationship she has been a positive influence in my life. As she has lived her faith out loud, it has prompted me to more closely follow Jesus.

I also dedicate these Positive Ponderings to my son Phillip. I have had the opportunity to utilize the book of Pro-Verbs in raising him in the ways of the Lord.

INTRODUCTION

You are holding in your hands a book dedicated to another book, found within a collection of 66 books called The Bible. The book of Proverbs is a collection of wisdom from a father to a son that can be used as the words of wisdom from our Heavenly Father speaking to his earthly sons and daughters. Proverbs is a practical book that compares wisdom to foolishness, unrighteousness to righteousness, faithfulness to unfaithfulness; and over and over again it points out the principle of cause and effect. The Father speaks to us because He loves us.

> *"For God so loved the world* **(man, wo-man and hu-man…aka mankind…aka…the world)** *that He gave His only begotten Son, that whosoever* **(man, wo-man, hu-man, mankind, the world)** *should believe in Him should not perish, but have everlasting/eternal life."* [emphasis mine]
>
> John 3:16

The book of Proverbs is divided into 31 chapters, which works nicely for daily devotions since there are never more than 31 days in a month. This book will not be an in-depth study of Proverbs. Instead, it will glean from each chapter something to chew on throughout the day. Hopefully *this* book will be an incentive to read *the* book after the 31 days are over.

Strong's Exhaustive Concordance of the Bible defines a proverb this way:

Proverb: mâshâl (*maw-shawl'*) in some original sense of *superiority* in mental action; properly a pithy *maxim*, usually of a metaphorical nature; hence a *simile* (as an adage, poem, discourse): - byword, like, parable, proverb.

mâshal (*maw-shal'*) A primitive root; to *rule:* - (have, make to have) dominion, governor, X indeed, reign, (bear, cause to, have) rule (-ing, -r), have power.

When I see the word *proverb*, I think of *Pro-Verb*. *Pro* speaks of something *positive*, and *Verb* speaks of an *action word*. When I read the book of *Pro-Verbs*, I read *positive action words*. It is a book of *practical applications* of the principles of God.

The key to the cause and effect of these pro-verbs in my life hinges on the word, *if*. I can read about the principles; I can agree with the principles; I can even believe in the principles; but *if* I don't apply the principles, I open the door to the negative side of the cause and effect principle. *If* you do this/that will happen; *if* you don't do this/that will happen.

There is no option for doing nothing. Doing nothing opens the door for the negative to happen. By doing nothing, you are doing something *wrong*. As you read these ruminations on *positive action*, think about how you can practically *do* something. We're not talking about activity just for the sake of activity. We're talking about actively listening for the voice of God, then being obedient to obey His instructions.

… Pro-Verb Ponderings

THE RUMINATION PRINCIPLE

The subtitle of this book is *31 Ruminations on Positive Action*. I teach a Sunday school class called The Ruminators, where we study the Bible like a cow chews the cud. We call it, 'mooin' and chewin' on the Word of God.'

The class was started a few years ago when a group of us were working through *The Topical Memory System* by the Navigators. One verse we memorized was:

"This book of the law shall not depart from your mouth; but you shall meditate on it (the law) day and night, so that you might be careful to do according to all that is written in it. (for) Then you will make your way prosperous and then you will have good success."

Joshua 1:8

Meditate: hâgâh (*haw-gaw'*) A primitive root; to *murmur* (in pleasure or anger); by implication to *ponder:* - imagine, meditate, mourn, mutter, roar, speak, study, talk, utter. [Strong's]

Ruminate comes from the Latin, *ruminatus,* which means *to chew the cud*. Animals that chew the cud are scientifically classified as ruminants. There are around 150 species of mammals that chew the cud including cows, goats, giraffes, yaks, antelopes, deer, llamas and sheep. The rumination process involves the animal chewing and swallowing its food. That food goes through a preliminary digestive process by passing through multiple stomach chambers before being regurgitated back up into the animal's mouth in the form of a *cud*, where it is chewed again to help complete the digestive process.

This is what we do with the Word of God (minus the four stomach chambers). We experience the Word of God, but that is not the end of the process. We keep the Word of God (our cud) in our mouths, as we *hagah* (haw-gaw) - *ruminate* - thus we become *ruminators*.

Before we begin the daily reading of the Proverbs, it might help you to determine how much you actually know about the book we are about to dive into. Here are a few questions to guide you in this self-examination:

Who wrote the book of Proverbs? (Proverbs 1:1, Proverbs 30:1; Proverbs 31:1)

_____

Who was Solomon's father? (Proverbs 1:1)

_____

Where and when did Solomon get this wisdom? (I Kings 3:5-14)

_____

Name three things God gave Solomon. (I Kings 4:29)

_____

_____

_____

How vast was this God-given wisdom? (I Kings 4:29-31)

_____

Pro-Verb Ponderings

How many Pro-Verbs did Solomon speak? (I Kings 4:32)

_____

How many songs did he write? (I Kings 4:32)

_____

Who came to hear Solomon? What did they come to hear? (I Kings 4:34)

_____

_____

What will you know? (Proverbs 1:2)

_____

What will you discern? (Proverbs 1:2)

_____

In what four things will you receive instruction? (Proverbs 1:3)

_____

_____

_____

_____

What will the naïve/simple ones receive? (Proverbs 1:4)

_____

What two things will the youth receive? (Proverbs 1:4)

_____

_____

What will the wise man hear and increase in? (Proverbs 1:5)

_____

What will a man of understanding acquire? (Proverbs 1:5)

_____

What four things will a wise man understand? (Proverbs 1:6)

_____

_____

_____

_____

What is the beginning of knowledge? (Proverbs 1:7)

_____

What two things do fools despise? (Proverbs 1:7)

_____

_____

Note: Which one are you: the fool who despises wisdom and instruction or the one who is at the beginning of knowledge, who fears the Lord?

Pro-Verb Ponderings

What are we to hear? (Proverbs 1:8)

_____

What are we not to forsake? (Proverbs 1:8)

_____

What two things will your father's instruction and your mother's teaching be to you? (Proverbs 1:9)

_____

_____

Now you are ready to delve in to this daily devotional. Keep your Bible by your side. Look up the Scriptures. Ruminate on the Word. Then take *positive action* in your daily, nitty-gritty, marketplace life.

Rodney Boyd

PRO-VERBS 1

Proverbs 1:9-19
Just Say No

In this world that we live, breathe and walk in, there are many voices crying out to you. Some are good; some are not so good. As you hear these voices, you will be presented with a choice: to go along with the voices or take a stand and not go along with the voices. I am convinced that temptation is not necessarily designed to pull you *into something* (although that will surely happen if you yield to temptation). Temptation is designed to *pull you away from who you really are*. There is a difference in being *tested* by God and *tempted* by the devil. A *testing* will strengthen you and draw you closer to God, while succumbing to *temptation* will separate you from God and weaken you, leaving you in a hovel of condemnation.

Who are the enticers? (Proverbs 1:10)

_____

_____

Entice: pâthâh (*paw-thaw'*) A primitive root; to *open*, that is, *be* (causatively *make*) *roomy*; usually figuratively (in a mental or moral sense) to *be* (causatively *make*) *simple* or (in a sinister way) *delude:* - allure, deceive, enlarge, entice, flatter, persuade, silly (one). [Strong's]

Pro-Verb Ponderings

What three little words does the Father recommend? (Proverbs 1:10)

_____

_____

_____

What are four examples of what the enticers might say? (Proverbs 1:11-12)

_____

_____

_____

_____

What reason do the enticers give for ambushing the innocent? (Proverbs 1:11)

_____

What kind of promises do the enticers give? (Proverbs 1:13-14)

_____

_____

_____

Along with the Father's advice, *do not consent,* what other advice does He give? (Proverbs 1:15)

_____

_____

_____

Where do their feet run? (Proverbs 1:16)

What do they hasten to do? (Proverbs 1:16)

What is it useless to do? (Proverbs 1:17)

> *Note: The enticers are lying in wait, in the shadows, waiting for the innocent. But in reality it will backfire on them - and you - if you choose to consent; throw in your lot with them; walk in the way with them; and put your feet on their path. You will be caught in the backfire.*

What does the enticer lie in wait for? (Proverbs 1:18)

What does the enticer ambush? (Proverbs 1:18)

What is the cause and effect of everyone who gains by violence? (Proverbs 1:19)

Pro-Verb Ponderings

This is a pretty good start on our 31-day journey through the Pro-Verbs. Three little words - *do not consent* - can change the course of our destiny. *Just say no* may seem simplistic, but how many bad things could I have avoided if I took heed to these words? In contrast to saying, *No*, to the enticers, we need to replace it with, *Yes*, to the Lord.

PRO-VERBS 2

Proverbs 2:1-5
Discerning and Discovering

In Proverb 1:7, we saw that, *"The fear of the Lord is the beginning of knowledge; Fools despise wisdom and instruction."* This wisdom and instruction in the Pro-Verbs comes from the Father and it is up to us to *choose* to enter into this "fear of the Lord." There are eight things that we must do as we set ourselves up for *discerning* and *discovering*. These things will not just drop in our laps and we will not attain them by osmosis. Proverbs 2:1 starts with the hinge word, *if*. *If* you do these things, certain things *will* happen. *If* you don't do these things, certain things will *not* happen.

What must we first do with the sayings of the Father? (Proverbs 2:1)

Receive: laqach *(law-kakh')* A primitive root; to *take* (in the widest variety of applications): - accept, bring, buy, carry away, drawn, fetch, get, infold, X many, mingle, place, receive (-ing), reserve, seize, send for, take (away, -ing, up), use, win. [Strong's]

When Jesus - who was God in the flesh - came down from glory, we are told that,

> *"He came to His own and those who were His own did not receive Him.*
>
> John 1:11

The same principle applies. Even though words of wisdom or The Word of God is presented to you, if you *don't receive*, it is of no effect in your life. It is hinged on *if* you *receive* or *if* you *don't receive*. The cause and effect principle applies.

> *"But as many as received Him, to them He gave the right to become children of God, even to those who believe in His name."*
>
> John 1:12

We can expect the *right* to *discern* the fear of the Lord and *discover* the knowledge of God, *if* we first *receive* the Father's sayings.

What are we to do with the Father's commandments? (Proverbs 2:1)

Treasure/Hide: tsaphan (*tsaw-fan'*) A primitive root; to *hide* (by *covering* over); by implication to *hoard* or *reserve*; figuratively to *deny*; specifically (favorably) to *protect*, (unfavorably) to *lurk:* - esteem, hide (-den one, self), lay up, lurk (be set) privily, (keep) secret (-ly, place). [Strong's]

When you receive the "seed of the Word," the attacks come to snatch it away, choke it out, dry it up, make it of no effect in your life. (Read Mark 4:1-20 and Luke 8:4-15 for the parable of the seed/sower/soil). We must guard the Words of the Father in our lives.

Where do we treasure/hide/guard the Father's commandments? (Proverbs 2:1)

What are we to do with our ears? (Proverbs 2:2)

We can hear people speak all day long but never *hear* what they say. We have to go from the physical act of hearing sound to *listening* and being *attentive*. In the physical, when we can't hear, we cup the outer ear so we can better funnel sound into our ears. We must do the same thing with our spirit (human spirit) ears; become *attentive* and *apply* to what the Father is saying.

Incline: qashab (*kaw-shab'*) A primitive root; to *prick up* the ears, that is, *hearken:* - attend, (cause to) hear (-ken), give heed, incline, mark (well), regard. [Strong's]

Apply: natah (*naw-taw'*) A primitive root; to *stretch* or spread out; by implication to *bend* away (including moral deflection); used in a great variety of applications: - + afternoon, apply, bow (down, -ing), carry aside, decline, deliver, extend, go down, be gone, incline, intend, lay, let down, offer, outstretched, overthrown, pervert, pitch, prolong, put away, shew, spread (out), stretch (forth, out), take (aside), turn (aside, away), wrest, cause to yield. [Strong's]

What are we to do with our heart? (Proverbs 2:2)

Pro-Verb Ponderings

What should we cry for? (Proverbs 2:3)

Cry: qara' (*kaw-raw'*) A primitive root (rather identical with through the idea of *accosting* a person met); to *call* out to (that is, properly *address* by name, but used in a wide variety of applications): - bewray [self], that are bidden, call (for, forth, self, upon), cry (unto), (be) famous, guest, invite, mention, (give) name, preach, (make) proclaim (-ation), pronounce, publish, read, renowned, say. [Strong's]

This is not just a faint calling out for discernment/knowledge, but an *accosting* - loud and emphatic - for what you want.

What are we to do for understanding? (Proverbs 2:3)

Again, it is not a quiet request; the voice is *lifted up* and *calling out*.

What two words are we to *do* regarding wisdom? (Proverbs 2:4)

> *Note: The word 'then' implies cause and effect if you seek understanding and discernment as silver and hidden treasure; as something very precious and valuable; not just something common.*

What will you *discern*? (Proverbs 2:5)

Fear: yir'âh *(yir-aw')* *fear* (also used as infinitive); morally *reverence:* - X dreadful, X exceedingly, fear (-fulness). [Strong's]

What will we *discover?* (Proverbs 2:5)

Pro-Verb Ponderings

We are encouraged by the Apostle Paul to work out our own - not someone else's, but our own - salvation with *fear* and *trembling*. To do this, we need to begin to:

- Receive
- Treasure
- Be attentive
- Incline our heart
- Cry out
- Lift our voice
- Seek
- Search

These are *positive action words* - Pro-Verbs that will have rich cause and effect as we work out our own salvation.

Day Two in our 31-day journey through the Pro-Verbs has us taking it up a notch in our actions to hear God. See ya on Day Three.

PRO-VERBS 3

Proverbs 3:1-12
Remember and Treasure

Memory can be defined as the storage of information and the recall of that information when needed in the absence of the original stimulus. The Father has called us to *not* forget his teaching and to allow our hearts to keep His commandments. We will see that there is great cause and effect promised if we do these things. If I don't keep these memories fresh - think about them, *ruminate* on them - I tend to forget. Combine that with the distractions and attacks on the teachings of the Father; I forget. The call is to *not forget* and to *treasure*.

As sons and daughters what are we *not* to forget? (Proverbs 3:1)

Forget: shakach, shakeach (*shaw-kakh', shaw-kay'-akh*) A primitive root; to *mislay*, that is, to *be oblivious* of, from want of memory or attention: - X at all, (cause to) forget. [Strong's]

What are we to do with the Father's commandments? (Proverbs 3:1)

Keep: nâtsar *(naw-tsar)'* A primitive root; to *guard*, in a good sense (to *protect, maintain, obey,* etc.) or a bad one (to *conceal,* etc.): - besieged, hidden thing, keep (-er, -ing), monument, observe, preserve (-r), subtil, watcher (-man). [Strong's]

Where are we to keep/guard/protect/maintain/obey these commandments? (Proverbs 3:1)

_____

What three things will be added if you don't forget the Father's teaching and keep/guard His commandments? (Proverbs 3:2)

_____

_____

_____

What are we *not* to *allow* to leave us? (Proverbs 3:3)

_____

Mercy: chesed *(kheh'-sed) kindness*; by implication (towards God) *piety*; rarely (by opprobrium) *reproof,* or (subjectively) *beauty:* - favour, good deed (-liness, -ness), kindly, (loving-) kindness, merciful (kindness), mercy, pity, reproach, wicked thing. [Strong's]

Kindness: chesed *(kheh'-sed) kindness*; by implication (towards God) *piety*; rarely (by opprobrium) *reproof,* or (subjectively) *beauty:* - favour, good deed (-liness, -ness), kindly, (loving-) kindness, merciful (kindness), mercy, pity, reproach, wicked thing. [Strong's]

Truth: 'emeth (*eh'-meth*) *stability*; figuratively *certainty, truth, trustworthiness:* - assured (-ly), establishment, faithful, right, sure, true (-ly, -th), verity. [Strong's]

> *Note: Truth is not just an assimilation of facts. Jesus told the woman at the well that true worshipers will worship in spirit and truth and that the Father is seeking such people to be His worshipers. He defined that God is Spirit; and those who worship him must worship in spirit (human) and in truth. (John 4:20-24)*
>
> *Later, at the Feast of Tabernacles Jesus spoke of Living Waters flowing out of our bellies - and He was speaking of the Holy Spirit - flowing out of our human spirits. (John 7:37-39) Jesus was teaching again; and many believed. He told them that if they would continue in Him, be his true disciples, then they would know the truth and that known truth will set them free. (John 8:30-36)*
>
> *Later still, Jesus would be praying to the Father - asking for certain things for His followers - and He defined truth. He prayed, "...sanctify them in truth; Thy Word is truth." (John 17:17)*

What two ways can we use to *not* allow them to leave us? (Proverbs 3:3)

_____

_____

The word *so* implies cause and effect. What will be the cause and effect? What will you find in binding and writing kindness and truth around your neck and in your heart? (Proverbs 3:4)

_____

Where will this favor and good repute/report be seen? (Proverbs 3:4)

Note: If you do nothing, then the teachings and commandments will be forgotten. We have seen that we are actively involved in the keeping process by binding them around our neck and writing them on the tablet of our hearts. The cause and effect will be manifest before God and man. The next few questions will explore the action - the things that we can do - that will ensure keeping kindness and truth around us.

In Whom are we to trust? (Proverbs 3:5)

Trust: bâtach (*baw-takh'*) A primitive root; properly to *hide* for refuge figuratively to *trust*, be *confident* or *sure:* - be bold (confident, secure, sure), careless (one, woman), put confidence, (make to) hope, (put, make to) trust. [Strong's]

How much of our hearts are we to use for trusting the Lord? (Proverbs 3:5)

What should we *not* lean on as we are trusting the Lord with all of our hearts? (Proverbs 3:5)

What are we to do in *all* our *ways*? (Proverbs 3:6)

What will be the *cause* and *effect* of you acknowledging Him in *all* your *ways*? (Proverbs 3:6)

What should we *not* be in our *own* eyes? (Proverbs 3:7)

> Note: Proverbs speaks of how we view our own way. "There is a way which seems right to a man, but its end is the way of death/destruction." (Proverbs 14:12/16:25) We see that "...the fool is right in his own eyes..." (Proverbs 12:15) "Every man's way is right in his own eyes, but the Lord weighs the hearts." (Proverbs 21:2) It's all about the heart of the matter.

How can we *not* be wise in our own eyes? (Proverbs 3:7)

What will be the cause and effect of fearing the Lord and turning from evil? (Proverbs 3:8)

Health/Healing: riph'ûth *(rif-ooth')* a *cure:* - health. râpha' râphâh *(raw-faw', raw-faw')* A primitive root; properly to *mend* (by stitching), that is, (figuratively) to *cure:* - cure, (cause to) heal, physician, repair, X thoroughly, make whole. [Strong's]

Marrow/refreshment: shiqquŷ *(shik-koo'ee)* a *beverage; moisture*, that is, (figuratively) *refreshment:* - drink, marrow. [Strong's]

Pro-Verb Ponderings

Where will this healing and refreshing be located? (Proverbs 3:7)

Body/Navel: shôr (*shore*) a *string* (as *twisted*), that is, (specifically) the umbilical cord (also figuratively as the centre of strength): - navel. [Strong's]

Bones: 'etsem (*eh'-tsem*) a *bone* (as *strong*); by extension the *body*; figuratively the *substance*, that is, (as pronoun) *selfsame:* - body, bone, X life, (self-) same, strength, X very. [Strong's]

Pro-Verb Ponderings

Healing and refreshing from keeping and treasuring teachings and commandments are ours. The next step in our journey will show us how *not* to be *footloose*.

See ya tomorrow for Day Four on the road to positive action.

PRO-VERBS 4

Proverbs 4:20-27
Footloose

Footing is everything. If you don't have good footing, you lose your balance and, *Boom!* - you fall down. This is true in simple walking and it is true in karate. In karate, *The Stance,* is what everything is built on for you to be able to throw a good technique. The stance, the posture, then the technique is needed for life also; and it all starts with the foot. The word for Kingdom - as in the Kingdom of God - is based on a word meaning foot/foundation. Pro-Verbs underscores this as we see how to get a good foundation with 12 Steps - 12 Positive Actions (aka Pro-Verbs) to a good foundation.

What are we to *give* to the Father's words? (Proverbs 4:20)

___

What position should our ears be inclined to from the Father? (Proverbs 4:20)

___

What should we keep in our sight? (Proverbs 4:21)

___

Note: Notice that we are not to allow these things to depart. If we allow it to happen, they will depart.

Where are we to *keep/guard* these things? (Proverbs 4:21)

Why should we give attention, incline our ears, not let/allow them to depart from our sight, keep them in the midst of our hearts? (Proverbs 4:22)

What are these things to those who find them? (Proverbs 4:22)

What is the benefit for the whole body when we find them? (Proverbs 4:22)

What are we to watch over? (Proverbs 4:23)

How are we to watch over our hearts? (Proverbs 4:23)

What flows from our watched-over hearts? (Proverbs 4:23)

Note: Jesus spoke of a heart where living waters flowed out of the belly, the innermost being. This flow was linked to drinking of Jesus and believing in Him. Is it any wonder we are called to watch over our belly, our innermost being, our heart? We don't want anything to happen to the flow.

What are we to put away from ourselves? (Proverbs 4:24)

_____

What should be put *far* away from us? (Proverbs 4:24)

_____

In which direction should your eyes be looking? (Proverbs 4:25)

_____

Where should your gaze be fixed? (Proverbs 4:25)

_____

What should we be watching? (Proverbs 4:26)

_____

What will be the cause and effect of watching the path of your feet? (Proverbs 4:26)

_____

Which way should we turn on the path? (Proverbs 4:27)

_____

What should we turn our foot from? (Proverbs 4:27)

_____

Note: The cause and effect in this Pro-Verb section is:

> *Life*
> *Health*
> *Flowing springs*
> *Established ways.*

These are all hinged on Positive Action that we take by:

> *Giving attention to the Father's words*
> *Inclining our ears to His sayings*
> *Not letting His words and sayings depart from our ears and eyes*
> *Keeping/Guarding His words and sayings in our heart, our innermost being*
> *Putting away a deceitful mouth*
> *Putting devious lips far from us*
> *Letting/allowing our eyes look directly ahead*
> *Letting/allowing our gaze to be fixed straight ahead*
> *Watching the path we walk*
> *Not turning right or left on the path we are on*
> *Turning our feet (where we walk) from evil*

All of these are choices. Choosing to not listen to and obey the Father also has cause and effect; the exact opposite of obeying:

> *Death*
> *Sickness*
> *Dammed up flow of springs*
> *Shaky and crumbling ways*

Pro-Verb Ponderings

We can either stand in faith or stand in doubt. Either stand will establish us in one or the other. Be loose in the footing and you will be established in looseness. Be strong in your footing and you will be established in strength.

Day Five continues. I hope you are enjoying the journey.

Rodney Boyd

PRO-VERBS 5

Proverbs 5:15-23
How To Avoid Trouble

A wise man once said, "Life is hard. It's harder when you're stupid." That is a true statement. Why add to the mess of life by doing something that will cause more trouble? In many of the Pro-Verbs, the Father uses 'the strange woman,' 'the harlot,' 'the adulteress' as the one who entices you into trouble by pulling you away from who you really are. Here the Father gives the son sound advice about avoiding trouble.

Whose cistern should you drink water from? (Proverbs 5:15)

Where should you drink running water from? (Proverbs 5:15)

Note: The well of running water is the source and the cistern is the place of storage of the water.

Should your fountains be dispersed abroad? (Proverbs 5:16)

Pro-Verb Ponderings

Should streams/channel of your water be in the streets? (Proverbs 5:16)

Note: Water speaks of life, vitality, refreshing, strength. Should your vitality be dispersed abroad or running out to the streets? No!

For whom should your water and your fountains be? (Proverbs 5:17)

Should your water and fountains be for strangers? (Proverbs 5:17)

What spiritual condition should your fountain be? (Proverbs 5:18)

With whom should we rejoice? (Proverbs 5:18)

Note: Now we get to the crux of the matter. Faithfulness. We will see how to avoid trouble by being faithful to your spouse.

What two objects represent the breasts of your wife? (Proverbs 5:19)

Note: Read Song of Solomon - the Song of Songs - for full details of how to love your wife.

What should we always be with her love? (Proverbs 5:19)

Note: We are told to be enraptured – intoxicated - with water from your own cistern and flowing waters from your own fountains. When you start drinking from other places you open the door to trouble. Men, stay at home!

In contrast to be enraptured/intoxicated with your *own* wife, who should you not be enraptured and intoxicated with? (Proverbs 5:20)

Where should you not be embraced? (Proverbs 5:20)

Note: The Pro-Verbist is using a father/son conversation about being faithful to your wife, by using the example of keeping your water source and supply pure and not opening up to the poison of strange waters. The larger implication and application is remaining faithful to the Lord.

The ways of man are in full view before Whom? (Proverbs 5:21)

Note: Watchman Nee said that if we really believe that Jesus resides within us by the Holy Spirit, we would not do or say the things that we do. There is nothing hidden from the Lord. Adam and Eve drank from strange waters and then tried to cover up and hide from God. What are you hiding from God? What strange waters are you drinking from that you think are hidden from God?

What does God ponder? (Proverbs 5:21)

What entraps the wicked man? (Proverbs 5:22)

Where is the wicked man caught? (Proverbs 5:22)

What is the two-fold cause and effect of this sin? (Proverbs 5:23)

Rodney Boyd

Pro-Verb Ponderings

Trouble is waiting for the person who drinks *strange waters*, instead of staying home and drinking from the *faithful waters of the Lord*.

Continued blessings on your journey into the land of Pro-Verbs.

PRO-VERBS 6

Proverbs 6:16-19
The Lord of Hate

We all know that the Lord is not the author of confusion, although He did confuse the people at the tower of Babel. He is not the God of fear, as perfect love casts out fear. He is Spirit - but became flesh and dwelt among us in the form of Jesus - and *He is Love*. He *loves* the world, but He does *hate*. Now, don't get all bent out of shape. God does not hate as the world hates, but He does *hate*. Pro-Verbs enumerates what the Lord *hates*. Let's us look at the six things the Lord *hates;* yes, *seven* that are an *abomination* to Him.

How many things does the Lord hate? (Proverbs 6:16)

Hate: śane' *(saw-nay)'* A primitive root; to *hate* (personally): - enemy, foe, (be) hate (-ful, -r), odious, X utterly. [Strong's]

How many things are an abomination to the Lord? (Proverbs 6:16)

Abomination: toʻebah toʻebah *(to-ay-baw', to-ay-baw')* properly something *disgusting* (morally), that is, (as noun) an *abhorrence*; especially *idolatry* or (concretely) an *idol*: - abominable (custom, thing), abomination. [Strong's]

> Note: Now we know that there are things that God considers to be an enemy, a foe, odious to Him and are actually disgusting to Him. If they are an abomination to Him, how should we feel about them and react to them?

What type of look does God hate and find disgusting? (Proverbs 6:17)

Proud: rum *(room)* A primitive root; to *be high* actively to *rise* or *raise* (in various applications, literally or figuratively): - bring up, exalt (self), extol, give, go up, haughty, heave (up), (be, lift up on, make on, set up on, too) high (-er, one), hold up, levy, lift (-er) up, (be) lofty, (X a-) loud, mount up, offer (up), + presumptuously, (be) promote (-ion), proud, set up, tall (-er), take (away, off, up), breed worms. [Strong's]

Pride: ga'on *(gaw-ohn')* - arrogancy, excellency (-lent), majesty, pomp, pride, proud, swelling. [Strong's]

What is the solution for pride? (I Peter 5:5-6)

What goes before destruction? (Proverbs 16:18)

What goes before a fall? (Proverbs 16:18)

Note: The Lord will not endure one who has a haughty look and a proud heart.

What type of tongue does the Lord hate? (Proverbs 6:17)

Lying: sheqer *(sheh'-ker)* an *untruth*; by implication a *sham* (often adverbially): - without a cause, deceit (-ful), false (-hood, -ly), feignedly, liar, + lie, lying, vain (thing), wrongfully. [Strong's]

Note: The tongue is merely the delivery system for the lie. The lie is within the heart. To counter the lie, you must speak the truth.

What is truth? (John 17:17)

What type of hands does the Lord hate? (Proverbs 6:17)

Note: The hands were made to heal not kill. One of the foundational doctrines is the laying on of hands. (Hebrews 6:2)

What type of heart does God hate? (Proverbs 6:18)

What type of feet does God hate? (Proverbs 6:18)

Note: God hates a false witness.

What does a false witness utter? (Proverbs 6:19)

_____

What does God not like to be spread among the brothers? (Proverbs 6:19)

_____

Pro-Verb Ponderings

Well, we have a partial list of things that God hates. When He says that there are six things which the Lord hates – yes, seven which are an abomination to Him - the wise Pro-Verbist means that the list *is specific* but *not exhaustive*:

Haughty *eyes*
A lying *tongue*
Hands that shed innocent blood
A *heart* that devises wicked plans
Feet that run rapidly to evil
A false *witness* who utters lies
And *one* who spreads strife among the brothers.

The question for me would be, "Are the body parts - of the One (aka *me*) - out of control or under control of the Father?

PRO-VERBS 7

Proverbs 7:6-27
Sudden Slaughter, Not So Sudden

This could be one of my *fav-o-rite* Pro-Verbs. It speaks of a naïve young man among the youth who begins a walk down to Sheol, i.e. *destruction*. So many times, we see people go up in flames and crash in their misery, and it appears to just happen out of the blue. In reality, the end result may come on suddenly, but it was building up for a while. Remember that temptation is not designed to pull you *into* something, as much as it is designed to pull you *away* from who you really are.

Where was the Pro-Verbist? What was he looking through? (Proverbs 7:6)

_____

_____

What type of young man did he see among the youth? (Proverbs 7:7)

_____

This young man was "among the youth." Why did this young man stand out? (Proverbs 7:7

_____

Pro-Verb Ponderings

What was this young man near as he was passing through the streets? (Proverbs 7:8)

> *Note: This is the first encounter as we see him coming near "her" corner. This was in "her" territory. This may be an innocent encounter but, if you don't "nip it in the bud," it can turn into a deeper encounter. So it is with us, as we brush up against enticement, temptation and sin in our "passing through the street" of life. "Her/She" is the adulteress.*

What is the next point of encounter? (Proverbs 7:8)

Where was he going? (Proverbs 7:8)

> *Note: This is now more than a chance encounter; it is now a matter of choice. He is beginning to get closer to the edge of the river bank and opening himself up for the possibility of slipping into the river of death. Also notice the transition from the street corner to her house and the time of day/night that he seeks her out.*

What four aspects of his time frame are mentioned? (Proverbs 7:9)

Who comes to meet him *out of her house*? (Proverbs 7:10)

___

What was this woman dressed as? (Proverbs 7:10)

___

What was the nature of her heart? (Proverbs 7:10)

___

What is her outward persona? (Proverbs 7:11)

___

Where do her feet not remain? (Proverbs 7:11)

___

What three places does she go when her feet do not remain at home? (Proverbs 7:12)

___

___

___

Lurk/Lie in Wait 'ârab (*aw-rab'*) A primitive root; to *lurk:* - (lie in) ambush (-ment), lay (lie in) wait. [Strong's]

> *Note: Now we begin to see the adulteress' tactics. In the movie, "Jailhouse Rock," Elvis grabbed the girl and kissed her. She responded, "Don't use those tactics on me." Elvis said, "Dem ain't tactics. That's just the beast in me." According to the Notes in the Ryrie Study Bible, The adulteress' tactics include:*

Kisses
Flattery
Sensuality
Reassurance

These all appeal to the flesh.

What physical tactic did she use to set up for the kiss? (Proverbs 7:13)

Note: The young man is in close enough proximity that she can reach out and touch him, seize him and pull him to her face to face. Now that's close!

What did she do when she seized him? (Proverbs 7:13)

What is the nature of her face, that he was so close to? (Proverbs 7:13)

Brazen: 'âzaz *(aw-zaz')* A primitive root; to *be stout* (literally or figuratively): - harden, impudent, prevail, strengthen (self), be strong. [Strong's]

What religious act was she due to offer? (Proverbs 7:14; Leviticus 7:11; Leviticus 7:16)

What had she paid on that day? (Proverbs 7:14)

Note: Verse 15 begins with "therefore," - which means that you are to see what it is "there for" - and refers back to the previous statement. Since I have performed my religious duties, therefore I have come to meet you. Possibly to eat the remaining meat on hand from the offerings (Leviticus 7:12-17) There is nothing worse than sin covered by religious acts.

What had she come out to do? (Proverbs 7:15)

What was she seeking? (Proverbs 7:15)

How intently had she sought out his presence? (Proverbs 7:15)

Note: Observe the beginning of stroking his ego. "I have come out to meet you, to seek your presence earnestly and I have found you." You can almost see his chest puff up and sniffing his nose like Barney Fife.

What two things had she done to entice him, to tempt him, to come into her bedroom? (Proverbs 7:16)

Where were the coverings and colored linens from? (Proverbs 7:16)

Pro-Verb Ponderings

What was her bed sprinkled with? (Proverbs 7:17)

___

Note: She is appealing to his senses of sight and smell. The trap is now set.

With this bed/couch adorned with coverings of colored linens from Egypt, and the smells of myrrh, aloes and cinnamon, what did she now suggest they do on that bed? (Proverbs 7:18)

___

Who was *not* at home? (Proverbs 7:19)

___

Where had he gone? (Proverbs 7:19)

___

What had he taken with him? (Proverbs 7:20)

___

When will he return home? (Proverbs 7:20)

___

Note: Our naïve young man has gone from passing through the streets near her corner, to taking the way to her house under the cover of night, to getting close enough to her to seize him and kiss him, to meeting her outside her house. Notice the progressive nature of the trap. She is now ready to bring out the big guns to close the deal.

What did she use to entice him? (Proverbs 7:21)

Did she use just one thing to persuade him? If not, how many things did she use? (Proverbs 7:21)

What did she use to seduce him? (Proverbs 7:21)

> *Note: Her lips were not just for kissin'. They were for flattery. "Oh you are such a big, strong, handsome, stud muffin." (translation mine)*

How quickly did the naïve, young man follow the harlot/adulteress? (Proverbs 7:22)

> *Note: As we stated from the first of this study, suddenly was not so sudden. It was a climatic build up to this point. Oh, the following her may have seemed sudden, but it was point-by-point of yielding his will, and choosing to go with her. In the Song of Songs - the Song of Solomon - we read that it is the little foxes that spoil the vineyard.*
>
> *"Catch the foxes for us, the little foxes that are ruining the vineyards, while our vineyards are in blossom."*
>
> Song of Solomon 2:15

What little foxes are you yielding to?

Pro-Verb Ponderings

What three examples of *sudden* does the Pro-Verbist use to describe the naïve young man? (Proverbs 7:22-23)

_____

_____

_____

What does the naïve young man *not know*? (Proverbs 7:23)

_____

What two things did the Pro-Verbist/Father want the son to do so he will *learn* from this naïve young man? (Proverbs 7:24)

_____

_____

What did the Pro-Verbist/Father want his sons to listen and pay attention to? (Proverbs 7:24)

_____

What two bits of advice did the Pro-Verbist/Father give the sons? (Proverbs 7:25)

_____

_____

Note: Observe that the son could let - or could not let - his heart turn aside to her ways. It is a matter of choice that must be nipped in the bud, when the foxes are small and the vineyard is still safe. Straying implies aimless walking.

If we have a purpose - and act like we are going somewhere - people tend to leave us alone.

Note: There is cause and effect in our choices. Deuteronomy talks about choosing "life or death," "blessing or cursing." The naïve young man has choices; and so do you.

Would this naïve young man be her first victim to cast down and slay? (Proverbs 7:26)

What is her house the way to? (Proverbs 7:27)

Where does her house descend? (Proverbs 7:27)

Note: Remember, her house looked very enticing. Enter in. See the pretty colored linens from Egypt. Smell the aroma of spices wafting throughout the house. See the prime opportunities. But, it is like a carnival's fun house, without the fun. What should be a good time for the flesh, turns into passageways that turn dark and go down deep, and you never come out. You now realize you are in a House of Horrors.

Pro-Verb Ponderings

This Pro-Verb took a little longer that the others; but it is my favorite. I can relate to sudden destruction as I backslid (actually slid face-forward) and then scratched my head as I wondered how I got to that place. In retrospect, I can look back and see each step of compromise that brought me to the place of *sudden* destruction, which was really not *sudden,* but *progressive* in nature.

Pro-Verbs 8 is on the horizon. We get to see the blessings of the way-keepers.

PRO-VERBS 8

Proverbs 8:32-36
Blessed Are The Way Keepers

Proverbs 8 kicks it off with the word of Wisdom *personified*. Sometimes Wisdom is personified as a *woman*, while some theologians see the Christ as Wisdom. The bottom line is this thing called Wisdom is a desired thing. We see Wisdom with God prior to creation and actively involved in creation and that Wisdom rejoiced throughout creation. Today we will focus on Wisdom's desire for the sons to listen to *Lady Wisdom* about the *blessings* involved with Wisdom.

Verse 32 starts off with, "Now therefore." From verse 1 to verse 31 there are various indications of *who* and *what* wisdom was involved in. "Now therefore" brings us to Wisdom, or the Pro-Verbist/God, wanting to speak about *blessing*.

What was the desire for the sons to do? (Proverbs 8:32)

_____

Who is blessed? (Proverbs 8:32)

_____

Blessed: 'esher *(eh'-sher) happiness*; only in masculine plural construction as interjection, how *happy!*: - blessed, happy.

Pro-Verb Ponderings

'âshar 'âshêr *(aw-shar', aw-share)'* A primitive root; to *be straight* (used in the widest sense, especially to *be level, right, happy*); figuratively to *go forward, be honest, prosper:* - (call, be) bless (-ed, happy), go, guide, lead, relieve. [Strong's]

What three ways do the sons keep the ways of wisdom? (Proverbs 8:33)

___

___

___

Who is a blessed man? (Proverbs 8:34)

___

What is found when you find wisdom? (Proverbs 8:35)

___

When you find wisdom - and life - what do you obtain? (Proverbs 8:35)

___

What happens if you sin against wisdom? (Proverbs 8:36)

___

Who loves death? (Proverbs 8:36)

___

> *Note: Wisdom is here for us to experience, to point us to the Lord. We are called to listen to wisdom, keep wisdom's ways, heed wisdom's instructions, be wise and not neglect*

wisdom's way. The cause and effect is blessing. But even in the blessing, we still must listen, watch and wait; and we will find life and favor from the Lord. If we don't do these things, and instead fail to seek and pursue this thing called wisdom, the cause and effect is self-injury and death.

Pro-Verb Ponderings

Ah, *Lady Wisdom* has spoken and her finger is pointing towards the Creator of all wisdom, the Lord God. If we hear her words and perceive her lessons, our lives will be so much better. She is always speaking, but are we always listening, and not just hearing words of wisdom but perceiving and implementing the words into positive action?

Day 9 approaches for more opportunities to walk in positive actions. Each new step will lead us closer to the completed journey.

Rodney Boyd

PRO-VERBS 9

Proverbs 9:13-18
Stolen Waters and Secret Bread

In Proverbs 8, we saw how our relationship with Wisdom brings us blessing, but that blessing must be received and acted upon. Proverbs 9 continues the thought about wisdom - personified as a woman - who prepares a place and calls out to the naïve to turn into the prepared place, forsake folly and live, and then proceed in the way of understanding. We see that the *fear of the Lord* is the beginning of *Wisdom,* and the knowledge of the *Holy One* is understanding. Armed with wisdom and knowledge, you can stand against the folly of the *boisterous woman*. Stolen waters and secret bread may seem sweet for the moment if we do not have wisdom and understanding; but in the end, they are death.

What is the woman of folly? (Proverbs 9:13)

Boisterous: hâmâh (*haw-maw)'* A primitive root to *make a loud sound* (like English "hum"); by implication to *be in great commotion* or *tumult,* to *rage, war, moan, clamor:* - clamorous, concourse, cry aloud, be disquieted, loud, mourn, be moved, make a noise, rage, roar, sound, be troubled, make in tumult, tumultuous, be in an uproar. [Strong's]

Pro-Verb Ponderings

Naïve/Simple: pᵉthayûth (*peth-ah-yooth'*) *silliness* (that is, *seducibility*): - simple; pᵉthîy pethîy pᵉthâ'îy (*peth-ee', peh'-thee, peth-aw-ee'*) *silly* (that is, *seducible*): - foolish, simple (-icity, one). pâthâh (*paw-thaw*)' A primitive root; to *open*, that is, *be* (causatively *make*) *roomy*; usually figuratively (in a mental or moral sense) to *be* (causatively *make*) *simple* or (in a sinister way) *delude:* - allure, deceive, enlarge, entice, flatter, persuade, silly (one). Knows Nothing: Bal (*bal*) properly a *failure*; by implication *nothing*; usually (adverbially) *not* at all; also *lest:* - lest, neither, no, none, not (any), nothing. [Strong's]

Where does the woman of folly sit? (Proverbs 9:14)

What is the boisterous woman of folly doing as she sits at her doorway and the high places of the city? (Proverbs 9:15)

What are those who are passing by her house and the high places of the city doing? (Proverbs 9:15)

Note: This is how we are as we walk in the Lord; we are walking in this world, making our paths straight, and we pass by places in this world that entice us to get off of the straight path. Remember: temptation/enticement is not designed to pull us into something, but is designed to pull us away from who we really are; to distract us from our purpose and destiny.

Rodney Boyd

What does the boisterous woman of folly entice the naïve to do? (Proverbs 9:16)

_____

What does the boisterous woman of folly tell the naïve that *stolen water* is? (Proverbs 9:17)

_____

What does the boisterous woman of folly tell the naïve that *bread eaten in secret* is? (Proverbs 9:17)

_____

Note: Stolen waters and bread eaten in secret represents things that are not meant for us to partake in. This is what sin is. In this case, the imagery is a harlot, a hooker, a prostitute, who is enticing/tempting the naïve to come in and partake of her body. Wisdom will give us understanding to just say, "No."

What should our response be when sinners - including boisterous women of folly - *entice* us? (Proverbs 1:10)

_____

What should we not do if, "they lay out their scheme to run to evil and hasten to shed blood." (Proverbs 1:15)

_____

Who are the guests in the *boisterous woman's hotel of Sheol* (a.k.a. Holiday Sin)? (Proverbs 9:18)

_____

Pro-Verb Ponderings

Where are the boisterous woman of folly's guests located? (Proverbs 9:18)

Sheol/Hell/Hades: sh^e'ol *(sheh-ole', sheh-ole')* *hades* or the world of the dead (as if a subterranean *retreat*), including its accessories and inmates: - grave, hell, pit. [Strong's]

Pro-Verb Ponderings

Once again, Pro-Verbs – *positive action* - will steer us away from trouble. We are able to choose life or death, blessing or curse. If we allow wisdom, knowledge and understanding to lead us - and we fear the Lord - we can avoid death.

Get your hope (confident expectation) up for Day 10 as we check out our mouths.

Pro-Verb Ponderings

PROVERBS 10

Proverbs 10:6, 8, 10-11, 13-14, 18-21, 31-32
The Fountain of Life

Throughout the Book of Pro-Verbs, there are many references to speech, the mouth, the tongue, the lips, and the cause and effect of what we say. Speech is merely words, thought and expressed by our mouths. The old saying is, "Sticks and stones may break my bones, but words can never harm/hurt me." Well, the old saying is *wrong*. Words can wound, kill, destroy and leave someone emotionally crippled for life; or, they can give life, heal, build up. Today we will look at how the words of the righteous and the words of the unrighteous affect us and others.

What is on the head of the righteous? (Proverbs 10:6)

_____

What does the mouth of the wicked conceal? (Proverbs 10:6)

_____

What does the wise of heart receive? (Proverbs 10:8)

_____

What will the babbling fool come to? (Proverbs 10:8)

Note: Just because we have many words - babbling on - does not mean it is necessarily a good thing.

Babbling/Prattling: sâphâh sepheth *(saw-faw', sef-eth')* the idea of *termination*; the *lip* (as a natural boundary); by implication *language*; by analogy a *margin* (of a vessel, water, cloth, etc.): - band, bank, binding, border, brim, brink, edge, language, lip, prating, ([sea-]) shore, side, speech, talk, [vain] words. [Strong's]

What will the babbling fool come to? (Proverbs 10:10)

What is the mouth of the righteous? (Proverbs 10:11)

What does the mouth of the wicked conceal? (Proverbs 10:11)

What does this violent hatred stir up? (Proverbs 10:12)

What does love cover? (Proverbs 10:12)

Love: 'ahăbâh *(a-hab-aw')* Feminine and meaning the same: - love. Ahab *(ah'-hab) affection* (in a good or a bad sense): - love (-r). 'âhab 'âhêb *aw-hab', aw-habe'* A primitive root; to

Pro-Verb Ponderings

have affection for (sexually or otherwise): - (be-) love (-d, -ly, -r), like, friend. [Strong's]

What is found on the lips of the discerning? (Proverbs 10:13)

___

What is reserved for the back of him who lacks understanding? (Proverbs 10:13)

___

What do wise men store up? (Proverbs 10:14)

___

What is at hand for the mouth of the foolish? (Proverbs 10:14)

___

> *Note: The wise man stores up in his heart and renewed mind so that what he speaks is not the same thing the mouth of the foolish speaks. The cause and effect for the wise will not be the same thing that is for the foolish.*

Who has lying lips? (Proverbs 10:18)

___

What is someone who spreads slander with those lying lips? (Proverbs 10:18)

___

What is unavoidable when many words are used? (Proverbs 10:19)

___

Who is considered to be wise? (Proverbs 10:19)

___

> *Note: In the Ruminator Sunday School class, we have a saying:*
>
> *"Unrestrained thoughts (what we think) produces unrestrained words (what we say) resulting in unrestrained actions (what we do)."*
>
> *When we don't restrain our lips - and let many words flow - sin is unavoidable. But he who restrains what he is thinking - at the lipgate — he is wise.*

What is the value of the righteous tongue? (Proverbs 10:20)

___

What is the value of the wicked heart? (Proverbs 10:20)

___

What will the lips of the righteous do? (Proverbs 10:21)

___

Why do fools die? (Proverbs 10:21)

___

What flows from the mouth of the righteous? (Proverbs 10:31)

What will happen to the perverted tongue? (Proverbs 10:31)

Perverted: tahpukah *(tah-poo-kaw') perversity* or *fraud:* - (very) froward (-ness, thing), perverse thing. hâphak *(haw-vak')* A primitive root; to *turn* about or over; by implication to *change, overturn, return, pervert:* - X become, change, come, be converted, give, make [a bed], overthrow (-turn), perverse, retire, tumble, turn (again, aside, back, to the contrary, every way). [Strong's]

What will the lips of the righteous bring forth? (Proverbs 10:32)

What will the mouth of the wicked bring forth? (Proverbs 10:32)

Pro-Verb Ponderings

The mouth reveals what is in the heart. I've got a feeling that we will be seeing more about the mouth and what we say in future Pro-Verbs.

Continue on fellow pilgrims as we walk in these Pro-Verb Ponderings. Day 11 awaits our arrival.

PRO-VERBS 11

Proverbs 11:24-29
Holy Financial Planning: a.k.a. God-o-nomics

In this crazy, swirling, whirling, roller coaster economy, Pro-Verbs gives out sound financial advice. This advice goes against the grain of the world system; but, it works. As with everything in the kingdom of God, it flows out of the heart, not the head. There is cause and effect in the kingdom of God that works for the good and works for the bad. It has been called seed faith, seed time and harvest, sowing and reaping, reciprocity. I call it *God-o-nomics*.

What are the two types of individuals? (Proverbs 11:24)

What happens to the one who scatters? (Proverbs 11:24)

What is the result of withholding that which is justly due? (Proverbs 11:24)

What does the withholder receive? (Proverbs 11:24)

What will the generous man be? (Proverbs 11:25)

What will be the cause and effect of the one who waters? (Proverbs 11:25)

GIVING AND RECEIVING
The Art of Abundance and Overflow
Bonus Rumination

What will happen when you give? (Luke 6:38)

Where will men pour into your bosom/lap/gathered clothing that forms a basket? (Luke 6:38)

What are the four levels of measurement? (Luke 6:38)

Note: Each level is designed to make room for more.

What will be the rule of measurement? (Luke 6:38)

Pro-Verb Ponderings

Note: This principle is not limited to money. Read Luke 6:20-38 for this sowing and reaping process.

SOWING AND REAPING

A New Testament underscoring of our Pro-Verb of the day.

What is the responsibility of the one who is taught? (Galatians 6:6)

___

What is God *not*? (Galatians 6:7)

___

If you mock God, what *are* you? (Galatians 6:7)

___

What happens when a man sows? (Galatians 6:7)

___

What are the limits to this sowing and reaping? (Galatians 6:7)

___

Note: Again this principle is not limited to finances, but is opened to whatever. The sowing will either be Spirit or flesh. One will have a harvest of corruption and the other will have a harvest of eternal life. The harvest of the reaper will be based on your choice of what you sow. (Galatians 6:7-8)

What is the time frame for reaping? (Galatians 6:9)

___

What should you not lose as you wait for the harvest? (Galatians 6:9)

What will you do *if* you do not grow weary? (Galatians 6:9)

What should we do while we have the opportunity? (Galatians 6:10)

What is the limit of who we sow goodness into? (Galatians 6:10)

Who are we to *especially* sow good to? (Galatians 6:10)

What will be the people's reaction to the one who *withholds* grain? (Proverbs 11:26)

What will be on the head of the one who does not *withhold*, but *sells* the grain? (Proverbs 11:26)

What is the one who diligently seeks good *really seeking*? (Proverbs 11:27)

Pro-Verb Ponderings

What will the evil seeker get in return for his evil seeking? (Proverbs 11:27)

What will happen to the one who trusts in his riches? (Proverbs 11:28)

What will the righteous flourish like? (Proverbs 11:28)

What will be the inheritance of the one who troubles his own house? (Proverbs 11:29)

Who will the foolish serve? (Proverbs 11:29)

What is the fruit of the righteous? (Proverbs 11:30)

What is the one who wins souls? (Proverbs 11:30)

Where will the righteous be rewarded? (Proverbs 11:31)

Who will be rewarded *much more* on earth?

Pro-Verb Ponderings

God-o-nomics is based on God's grace, mercy and love; but our withdrawal is based on, *hinged on,* our releasing, giving, scattering and generosity. For more on giving and receiving, see II Corinthians 9:6-15; Malachi 3:7-12; Luke 6:38; Galatians 6.

Sowing and Reaping leads to Fruits and Roots. 'Tis better to plant in positive soil than negative, hard, cracked, dry ground. Day 12 is on its way.

PRO-VERBS 12

Proverbs 12:3, 7, 12, 19
Established Roots and Fruits

Throughout Pro-Verbs there is a contrast between the righteous and the wicked; and so it is with Proverbs 12. The cause and effect of the wicked is obvious: destruction, death, rottenness, ensnarled, folly, anxiety, death and more. On the other side, the righteous cause and effect is established: fruit, healing, joy, delight, life, gladness and more. Today we want to look at the roots, fruits, establishment and more.

What will a man *not* be established by? (Proverbs 12:3)

Established: kûn (*koon*) A primitive root; properly to *be erect* (that is, stand perpendicular); hence (causatively) to *set up*, in a great variety of applications, whether literal (*establish, fix, prepare, apply*), or figurative (*appoint, render sure, proper* or *prosperous*): - certain (-ty), confirm, direct, faithfulness, fashion, fasten, firm, be fitted, be fixed, frame, be meet, ordain, order, perfect, (make) preparation, prepare (self), provide, make provision, (be, make) ready, right, set (aright, fast, forth), be stable, (e-) stablish, stand, tarry, X very deed.[Strong's]

What will cause the righteous to be established and *not* moved? (Proverbs 12:3)

___

Root: sheresh *(sheh'-resh)* a *root* (literally or figuratively): - bottom, deep, heel, root. shârash *(shaw-rash')* A primitive root; to *root*, that is, strike into the soil, or (by implication) to pluck from it: - (take, cause to take) root (out). [Strong's]

What will be the effect of the righteous when he is rooted? (Proverbs 12:3)

___

Will not be moved: môt *(mote')* A primitive root; to *waver*, by implication to *slip, shake, fall:* - be carried, cast, be out of course, be fallen in decay, X exceedingly, fall (-ing down), be (re-) moved, be ready shake, slide, slip. [Strong's]

Note: In the world that we live in, things are constantly shifting, changing, uprooting, falling down. But the righteous - those with right standing - have the promise of stability in the middle of the shaking. However, it is based on roots, establishment and foundation.

What three postures will the blessed man *not* assume? (Psalms 1:1)

Pro-Verb Ponderings

Blessed: 'esher *(eh'-sher) happiness*; only in masculine plural construction as interjection, how *happy!* - blessed, happy. 'âshar 'âshêr *(aw-shar', aw-share')* A primitive root; to *be straight* (used in the widest sense, especially to *be level, right, happy*); figuratively to *go forward, be honest, prosper:* - (call, be) bless (-ed, happy), go, guide, lead, relieve. [Strong's]

What three types of negative people should the blessed man not walk, stand or sit with or in? (Psalm 1:1)

___

___

___

Note: See the progression of being in the midst of the wicked, sinners, scoffers. It starts off by walking in their presence; then there is a stopping and standing in their pathways; and then sitting with them. If you do not do these things, you will be blessed.

What will the blessed man's delight be in? (Psalms 1:2)

___

Delight: chêphets *(khay'-fets) pleasure*; hence (abstractly) *desire*; concretely a *valuable* thing; hence (by extension) a *matter* (as something in mind): - acceptable, delight (-some), desire, things desired, matter, pleasant (-ure), purpose, willingly. châphêts *khaw-fates'* A primitive root; properly to *incline* to; by implication (literally but rarely) to *bend*; figuratively to *be pleased* with, *desire:* - X any at all, (have, take) delight, desire, favour, like, move, be (well) pleased, have pleasure, will, would. [Strong's]

What will the blessed man do in His law? (Psalm 1:2)

_____

Meditate: hâgâh (*haw-gaw'*) A primitive root; to *murmur* (in pleasure or anger); by implication to *ponder:* - imagine, meditate, mourn, mutter, roar, X sore, speak, study, talk, utter. In the Latin, to *Ruminate;* chew, mutter under breath - i.e. *moo and chew.*

What is the time frame for this meditation? (Psalms 1:2)

_____

What will be the four-fold cause and effect of *not* walking, standing, sitting in the counsel/path of the wicked, sinners and scoffers, *and* delighting in the law of the Lord and meditating day and night? (Psalms 1:3)

_____

_____

_____

_____

Note: In contrast, the wicked are not so. They become like chaff and are driven away by the wind (the opposite of being established when the winds come). The wicked will not stand in the judgment; the sinners will not stand in the assembly of the righteous. (Psalms 1:4-5)

What does the Lord know? (Psalm 1:6)

_____

Pro-Verb Ponderings

What will happen to the way of the wicked? (Psalms 1:6)

Note: This excursion in Psalm 1 was kicked off by the statement that the root of the righteous will not be moved. It is all hinged on where you are planted. Now back to the Pro-Verbs.

What are two end results of the wicked? (Proverbs 12:7)

What will be the end result of the house of the righteous? (Proverbs 12:7)

Note: We see that the house of the righteous will be established. That does not mean that we are immune to the storms of life but, when we are established - have a firm foundation -we will stand.

What relationship with *the words of Jesus* will cause a house to be built on *the Rock*? (Matthew 7:24)

What three things came against the house built on *the Rock*? (Matthew 7:25)

Did the house fall? (Matthew 7:25)

Why did the house *not fall*? (Matthew 7:25)

In contrast to the house built on *the Rock*, what will the one who does not act on the words that he hears be like? (Matthew 7:26)

> *Note: The same storm comes against the Rock foundation house and the Sand foundation house.*
>
> *Note: The storms comes against both houses. The one who stands will be the one with the firm, established foundation, which comes from hearing and acting on the words of Jesus.*
>
> *Note: I realize that we are straying from the Pro-Verb premise, but I feel these excursions underscore the Pro-Verbs concept.*
>
> *Note: I Corinthians 15:58 starts of with, "Therefore," and refers back to references about death and sin; and the loss of the sting of death=sin; and the power of sin=the law. It speaks of the victory through our Lord Jesus Christ; "Therefore." The "therefore" leads us in to what we should be.*

What four things should we be because of the *victory through our Lord Jesus Christ*? (I Corinthians 15:58)

Pro-Verb Ponderings

_____

_____

What should we always be abounding in? (I Corinthians 15:58)

_____

What should we know? (I Corinthians 15:58)

_____

Note: The link to Proverbs 12 is *establishment*.

What does the wicked man desire? (Proverbs 12:12)

_____

What does the *root of the righteous* yield? (Proverbs 12:13)

_____

What will a man be satisfied by? (Proverbs 12:14)

_____

What will return to a man? (Proverbs 12:14)

_____

What will be *established* forever? (Proverbs 12:19)

_____

What is only for a moment? (Proverbs 12:19)

_____

Pro-Verb Ponderings

What is spoken and what is done is how we *establish* ourselves. What we hear, what we meditate on, what we say and what we do - good or bad - will determine our end results. The Positive Action *Pro-Verbs* is to *restrain* what we think, what we say and what we do. Unrestrained thoughts - what we think - produces unrestrained words - what we say - resulting in unrestrained actions -what we do.

I am very aware that Day 13 is on its way. When you read Day 13's pondering, you will be aware also.

PRO-VERBS 13

Proverbs 13:3, 6
Be On The Zanshin

In Japanese karate, there is a word called, *Zanshin*. This word simply means, "awareness of your surroundings" or "be on guard." When you are walking from a mall to your car - whether at night or in the daytime -your mind should not be on automatic pilot. You should have your guard up, or your *zanshin* radar up, surveying the parking lot just in case there is someone lying in wait to attack you. This same principle works in your spiritual life.

What does a man/wo-man/hu-man enjoy? (Proverbs 13:2)

Good: tôb *(tobe) good* (as an adjective) in the widest sense; used likewise as a noun, both in the masculine and the feminine, the singular and the plural (*good*, a *good* or *good* thing, a *good* man or woman; the *good*, *goods* or *good* things, *good* men or women), also as an adverb (*well*): - beautiful, best, better, bountiful, cheerful, at ease, X fair (word), (be in) favour, fine, glad, good (deed, -lier, liest, -ly, -ness, -s), graciously, joyful, kindly, kindness, liketh (best), loving, merry, X most, pleasant, + pleaseth, pleasure, precious, prosperity, ready, sweet, wealth, welfare, (be) well ([-favoured]). tôb *(tobe)* A primitive root, to *be* (transitively *do* or *make*) *good* (or *well*) in the widest sense: - be (do) better, cheer, be (do, seem) good, (make), goodly, X please, (be, do, go, play) well. [Strong's]

Where does this enjoyed good come from? (Proverbs 13:2)

Fruit: p^{e}rîy (*per-ee'*) *fruit* (literally or figuratively): - bough, ([first-]) fruit ([-ful]), reward. pârâh (*paw-raw*)' A primitive root; to *bear fruit* (literally or figuratively): - bear, bring forth (fruit), (be, cause to be, make) fruitful, grow, increase. [Strong's]

What is the desire of the treacherous? (Proverbs 13:2)

Who preserves their lives? (Proverbs 13:3)

Guard/Keep: nâtsar (*naw-tsar'*): A primitive root; to *guard*, in a good sense (to *protect, maintain, obey*, etc.) or a bad one (to *conceal*, etc.): - besieged, hidden thing, keep (-er, -ing), monument, observe, preserve (-r), subtil, watcher (-man). [Strong's]

Guard: shâmar (*shaw-mar'*) A primitive root; properly *to hedge about (as with thorns)*, that is, *guard*; generally to *protect, attend to*, etc.: - beware, be circumspect, take heed (to self), keep (-er, self), mark, look narrowly, observe, preserve, regard, reserve, save (self), sure, (that lay) wait (for), watch (-man). [Strong's]

Pro-Verb Ponderings

Proverbs 13:3 *"He that* **keepeth** *(guards/natsar) his mouth* keepeth *(guards/shamar) his life: but he that openeth wide his lips shall have destruction."* [Strong's. emphasis mine]

How does someone come to ruin? (Proverbs 13:3)

Note: We have seen in past Pro-Verbs that unrestrained thoughts produce unrestrained words, resulting in unrestrained actions. There is cause and effect if we do not restrain - or guard - our MOUTHS. The mouth is the portal that reveals our heart, our thoughts.

Note: According to Proverbs 30:32, the place of foolish exaltation and plotting of evil is the mouth. We will ruminate on this when we get to Proverbs 30, but I encourage you take some time and read it now.

Note: There are outside forces that are on the attack of your heart and your mind. These areas also need guarding. Philippians 4 speaks of that guard.

Who is near? (Philippians 4:5)

What Pro-Verb should we be doing, since the Lord is near? (Philippians 4:4)

Since the Lord is near, what should we *not* be? (Philippians 4:6)

How much should we *not* be anxious about? (Philippians 4:6)

In contrast to the nothing – *no thing, nada, zip, zilch, zero* - what should be the amount that we pray, supplicate and thank Him for? (Philippians 4:6)

What three things should we be doing in everything? (Philippians 4:6)

Prayer: proseuchē *(pros-yoo-khay')* *prayer* *(worship)*; by implication an *oratory* *(chapel)*: - X pray earnestly, prayer. proseuchomai *(pros-yoo'-khom-ahee)* to *pray to* God, that is, *supplicate, worship:* - pray (X earnestly, for), make prayer. [Strong's]

This is talking to God; expressing need and conversational dialogue.

Supplication: deēsis *(deh'-ay-sis)* a *petition:* - prayer, request, supplication. deomai *(deh'-om-ahee)* to *beg* (as *binding oneself*), that is, *petition:* - beseech, pray (to), make request. [Strong's]

This is more than just asking; it is an impassioned listing, a specific need.

Thanksgiving: Eucharistia *(yoo-khar-is-tee'-ah) gratitude*; actually *grateful language* (to God, as an act of worship): - thankfulness, (giving of) thanks (-giving). Eucharistos *(yoo-khar'-is-tos) well favored*, that is, (by implication) *grateful*: - thankful. [Strong's]

This is thanking God for answered prayer *before* the answer appears.

What are we to let/allow to take place? (Philippians 4:6)

What calming presence will take place when we first *pray, supplicate, thank Him and allow/let our requests be made known to Him*? (Philippians 4:7)

Peace eirēnē *(i-rah'-nay)* Probably from a primary verb εἴρω eirō (to *join*); *peace* (literally or figuratively); by implication *prosperity:* - one, peace, quietness, rest, + set at one again. [Strong's]

What will this peace surpass? (Philippians 4:7)

All Understanding/Comprehension: nous *(nooce)* the *intellect*, that is, *mind* (divine or human; in thought, feeling or will); by implication *meaning*: - mind, understanding. [Strong's]

What two places will this comprehension surpassing peace be *guarding*? (Philippians 4:7)

Guard/Keep: phroureō *(froo-reh'-o)* to *be a watcher in advance*, that is, to *mount guard* as a sentinel (*post spies* at gates); figuratively to *hem in, protect*: - keep (with a garrison). pro *(pro)* A primary preposition; "fore", that is, *in front of, prior* (figuratively *superior*) *to*. In compounds it retains the same significations: - above, ago, before, or ever. In compounds it retains the same significations. horaō *(hor-ah'-o)* Properly to *stare* at that is, (by implication) to *discern* clearly (physically or mentally); by extension to *attend* to; by Hebraism to *experience*; passively to *appear*: - behold, perceive, see, take heed. [Strong's]

> Note: *The idea is like a Roman garrison; the toughest, elite soldiers guarding in front with a steely stare, discerning clearly and attending to, what is trying to penetrate to your heart and your mind. As we are talking about in Prov-Verbs, we need to be on guard – on zanshin - the awareness of our surroundings.*

Hearts: kardia *(kar-dee'-ah)* Prolonged from a primary καρ kar (Latin *cor*, "heart"); the *heart*, that is, (figuratively) the *thoughts* or *feelings* (*mind*); also (by analogy) the *middle*: - (+ broken-) heart(-ed). [Strong's]

Minds: noēma *(no'-ay-mah)* a *perception*, that is, *purpose*, or (by implication) the *intellect, disposition*, itself: - device, mind, thought. noieō *(noy-eh'-o)* to *exercise* the *mind* (*observe*), that is, (figuratively) to *comprehend, heed*: - consider, perceive, think, understand. nous *(noce)* the *intellect*, that is, *mind* (divine or human; in thought, feeling, or will); by implication *meaning*: - mind, understanding. [Strong's]

Where will this *guarding* of the heart and mind be found? (Philippians 4:7)

Pro-Verb Ponderings

Note: Part of the guarding process is hinged on what your mind is dwelling on. Where you are dwelling will be telling on your lips and in your actions. Read Philippians 4:8 for acceptable dwelling thoughts.

What guards the one whose way is blameless? (Proverbs 13:6)

_____

What subverts the sinner? (Proverbs 13:6)

_____

Pro-Verb Ponderings

When we let our *guard* down, we can go from blameless to sinner. This thing called *Zanshin* (awareness of your surroundings) is a practical, positive, state of mind that is not only good for your general environment, but also for your spiritual environment.

Day 14 takes us down on the farm with the sights, sounds and smells of the Kingdom. See ya there.

PRO-VERBS 14

Proverbs 14:4, 11-12, 23
Milk and Manure

"Milk does a body good," according to the Dairy Counsel. But what about the *manure* that is a by-product of milk production? We tend to look at such disturbances as an interruption to our lives; but it is just part of the process. Those who have no *mess* in their lives are probably not accomplishing much for the kingdom.

What is the condition of the manger when there are *no* oxen (i.e. *Ruminators - mooin' and chewin'*)? (Proverbs 14:4)

_____

What comes by the strength of the ox? (Proverbs 14:4)

_____

Revenue/Increase: tᵉbuʾah (*teb-oo-aw'*) *income*, that is, *produce* (literally or figuratively): - fruit, gain, increase, revenue. boʾ (*bo*) A primitive root; to *go* or *come* [Strong's]

> *Note: No oxen; no manure; no milk production; no revenue. Sometimes it gets messy when you are doing business in the natural; but that is part of the process. The oxen/cow eats the hay and produces the milk, but also produces the manure that makes things messy. The same goes for life in the Kingdom. We chew the Word of God;*

produce the fruit of the Spirit, gifts of the Spirit; feed others; feed ourselves; and we produce the manure of life, which is the doing-away with the unnecessary stuff that stinks and is messy. The alternative is to play it safe: don't eat the Word of God, don't be active in the Kingdom of God. The stall will be pristine, but our life will be useless.

What will be the end of the house of the wicked? (Proverbs 14:11)

What will be the future of the house of the upright? (Proverbs 14:11)

Note: The house represents our lives. Our lives will either be productive or non-productive. Our lives will either be destroyed or flourishing. It is all hinged on what we choose to do - how we conduct our lives, what we choose to allow in our lives - that will determine our future.

What seems right to a man/wo-man/hu-man? (Proverbs 14:12)

Way: bo' *(bo)* A primitive root; to *go* or *come*

What is the *end* to what we think is right? (Proverbs 14:12)

Note: We can believe all kinds of things about the way that we go or come in this life. We can be sincere, but we can be sincerely wrong. The end result will tell whether we were thinking right or wrong. One will be a destroyed house, the other will be a flourishing house. What we believe - what seems right - will affect the way we act, the way we work, the way we labor.

Where is profit? (Proverbs 14:23)

What will *mere talk* lead to? (Proverbs 14:23)

Pro-Verb Ponderings

Faith without works is dead, and good intentions without good labor are mere talk. We are called to have the rubber-meets-the-road intentions in the Kingdom of God. Pro-Verbs - Positive-Actions - will always end with profit in the Kingdom.

Tomorrow will take a look at the power of our words when we tend to shoot off our mouth. Wow, the Pro-Verbs are practical for every area of our lives.

PRO-VERBS 15

Proverbs 15:1-4; 13-14; 18; 26, 28
The .357 Caliber Mouth

"Sticks and stones may break my bones but words can never harm me." Nice sentiment, but bad theology. Words wound. Words cut deep. Words destroy. Words separate. Our mouths are like guns and our mouths shoot off with either kindness or hatred. The chamber is our heart loaded by what we think; and when you least expect it...Boom! We pull the trigger of our tongue and the word-bullets penetrate the hearts of the ones we aim at.

What turns away wrath? (Proverbs 15:1)

Soft: rak *(rak) tender* (literally or figuratively); by implication *weak:* - faint [-hearted], soft, tender ([-hearted], one), weak. râkak *(raw-kak')* A primitive root; to *soften* (intransitively or transitively), used figuratively: - (be) faint ([-hearted]), mollify, (be, make) soft (-er), be tender. [Strong's]

Answer: ma‛ăneh *(mah-an-eh')* a *reply* (favorable or contradictory): - answer, X himself. [Strong's]

What does a harsh word stir up? (Proverbs 15:1)

Harsh: ʿetseb *(ebʹ-tseb)* an earthen *vessel*; usually (painful) *toil*; also a *pang* (whether of body or mind): - grievous, idol, labor, sorrow. ʿâtsab *(aw-tsabʹ)* A primitive root; properly to *carve*, that is, *fabricate* or *fashion*; hence (in a bad sense) to *worry*, *pain* or *anger*: - displease, grieve, hurt, make, be sorry, vex, worship, wrest. [Strong's]

Anger: Aph *(af)* properly the *nose* or *nostril*; hence the *face* and occasionally a *person*; also (from the rapid breathing in passion) *ire:* - anger (-gry), + before, countenance, face, + forbearing, forehead, + [long-] suffering, nose, nostril, snout, X worthy, wrath. 'ânaph *(aw-naf)'* A primitive root; to *breathe* hard, that is, *be enraged:* - be angry (displeased). [Strong's]

Note: We are either going to be a wrath-turner or we are going to be an anger-stirrer-upper.

What does the tongue of the wise make? (Proverbs 15:2)

___

In contrast to the tongue of the wise, what do the mouths of fools spout? (Proverbs 15:2)

___

Where are the eyes of the Lord? (Proverbs 15:3)

___

What are the eyes of the Lord watching in every place? (Proverbs 15:3)

___

Pro-Verb Ponderings

What is a tree of life? (Proverb 15:4)

What happens when there is perversion in the tongue instead of soothing? (Proverbs 15:4)

What are the two types of tongues? (Proverbs 15:4)

Soothing/Wholesome: marpê' (*mar-pay'*) properly *curative*, that is, literally (concretely) a *medicine*, or (abstractly) a *cure*; figuratively (concretely) *deliverance*, or (abstractly) *placidity*: - ([in-]) cure (-able), healing (-lth), remedy, sound, wholesome, yielding. râphâ' râphah (*raw-faw', raw-faw'*) A primitive root; properly to *mend* (by stitching), that is, (figuratively) to *cure*: - cure, (cause to) heal, physician, repair, X thoroughly, make whole.

Perversion/Perverseness: Seleph (*seh'-lef*) *distortion*, that is, (figuratively) *viciousness:* - perverseness. sâlaph (*saw-laf*)' A primitive root; properly to *wrench*, that is, (figuratively) to *subvert:* - overthrow, pervert.

> *Note: One tongue heals, the other overthrows. When the tongue throws out words of kindness in a soft manner, there is a healing. When the tongue shoots off perverse words - words of strife and anger - there is a distortion and viciousness to them. It kills, or at the very least causes wounds that will be carried for the rest of the receiver's life.*

Rodney Boyd

What makes a cheerful face? (Proverbs 15:13)

What is broken when the heart is sad? (Proverbs 15:13)

What does the mind of the intelligent seek? (Proverbs 15:14)

What do the mouths of fools feed on? (Proverbs 15:14)

> *Note: What your mind dwells on will affect the way you carry yourself. If you are thinking about (ruminating, meditating on) folly, you will have a broken spirit. But if you focus on words of life, with true knowledge, then your spirit will not be broken, and your heart will reflect your face. That does not mean that you must always have a smile on your lips; but the tense, angry countenance will be replaced with a face of peace.*

What does a hot-tempered man stir up? (Proverbs 15:18)

> *Note: Remember Proverbs 15:1-4. We see how the harsh word stirs up anger, but a gentle answer turns away wrath. The hot-tempered man has been dwelling on harshness, strife, bitterness, resentment. He seethes, and explodes with his mouth.*

Pro-Verb Ponderings

Who can calm a dispute? (Proverbs 15:18)

___

What must we be quick to do? (James 1:19)

___

As we are quick to hear, what should we be slow to do? (James 1:19)

___

What else should we be slow to do? (James 1:19)

___

What does the anger of man *not* achieve? (James 1:20)

___

Note: James 1:21 starts off with, "Therefore," in reference to being swift to hear, slow to speak and slow to anger. What follows is how we can help to accomplish those three things.

What are we to put aside? (James 1:21)

___

What are we to receive in place of filthiness and wickedness? (James 1:21)

___

What attitude of reception should we have? (James 1:21)

___

What is this implanted *Word* able to do? (James 1:21)

What should we prove ourselves to be? (James 1:22)

What are we *not* to *merely* be? (James 1:22)

When you merely hear and don't do the word, what do you do to yourselves? (James 1:22)

> *Note: There is a direct correlation to the words that we hear and do, to how we are able to be swift to hear, slow to speak and slow to anger. It is what we are loading into the chambers of our heart that will exit through our mouth.*

What is an abomination to the Lord? (Proverbs 15:26)

What are pleasant words? (Proverbs 15:26)

What does the heart of the righteous ponder? (Proverbs 15:28)

What does the mouth of the wicked pour out? (Proverbs 15:28)

Pro-Verb Ponderings

What is the one who is *slow to anger* better than? (Proverbs 16:32)

___

What is one who rules his spirit (little 's' *human* spirit) better than? (Proverbs 16:32)

___

Pro-Verb Ponderings

Words will either be well thought-out, or just tripe pouring out of the mouth. Out of the abundance of the heart, the *mouth speaks*. If you carried around a tape recorder and recorded your words, what would you hear coming out of your mouth? Would you find yourself *killing* and *wounding* people around you, or *healing* and *helping* people? You can be mighty or angry. You can rule your spirit and be a better man or woman.

Make plans for tomorrow to check out how to make pleasing plans. Be blessed.

Pro-Verb Ponderings

PRO-VERBS 16

Proverbs 16:1-4, 7, 9, 18-20, 33
Pleasing Plans

We are a planet of goal-setters. In this world we live in, if you want to be a mover and shaker you have to plan ahead if you want to accomplish anything. We have financial planners. fitness planners, wedding planners and family planners just to name a few. But sometimes, the best laid plans of mice and men go astray, *if* our plans are not submitted to the Lord.

What belongs to man? (Proverbs 16:1)

Plans/Preparation: ma'ărâk *(mah-ar-awk')* an *arrangement*, that is, (figuratively) mental *disposition:* - preparation. ma'an *(mah'-an)* properly *heed*, that is, *purpose*; used only adverbially, *on account of* (as a motive or an aim), teleologically *in order that:* - because of, to the end (intent) that, for (to, 's sake), + lest, that, to. [Strong's]

Where does the answer of the tongue come from? (Proverbs 16:1)

What is clean in a man's own sight? (Proverbs 16:2)

Rodney Boyd

What does the Lord weigh? (Proverbs 16:2)

What are we called to commit to the Lord? (Proverbs 16:3)

What has the Lord made everything for? (Proverbs 16:4)

What does this include? (Proverbs 16:4)

What is the cause and effect of when a man's ways are pleasing to the Lord? (Proverbs 16:7)

What does the mind of man plan? (Proverbs 16:9)

What does the Lord direct? (Proverbs 16:9)

Note: We have plans, but the Lord can show us how to walk out those plans so they may be accomplished.

What goes before destruction? (Proverbs 16:18)

Pride: gâ'ôn (*gaw-ohn'*) arrogancy, excellency (-lent), majesty, pomp, pride, proud, swelling. [Strong's]

Destruction: sheber shêber *(sheh'-ber, shay'-ber)* a *fracture*, figuratively *ruin*; specifically a *solution* (of a dream): - affliction, breach, breaking, broken [-footed, -handed], bruise, crashing, destruction, hurt, interpretation, vexation. [Strong's]

Note: When we don't allow God to direct our steps in our plans, we are saying that we are big enough to accomplish it without God. That is nothing but pride. The cause and effect - destruction.

What goes before stumbling or a fall? (Proverbs 16:18)

Haughty: gôbahh *(go'-bah) elation, grandeur, arrogance:* - excellency, haughty, height, high, loftiness, pride. gâbahh *(gaw-bah')* A primitive root; to *soar*, that is, *be lofty*; figuratively to *be haughty:* - exalt, be haughty, be (make) high (-er), lift up, mount up, be proud, raise up great height, upward. [Strong's]

Fall: kishshalôn *(kish-shaw-lone')* properly a *tottering*, that is, *ruin:* - fall. kâshal *(kaw-shal')* A primitive root; to *totter* or *waver* (through weakness of the legs, especially the ankle); by implication to *falter, stumble,* faint or fall: - bereave [from the margin], cast down, be decayed, (cause to) fail, (cause, make to) fall (down, -ing), feeble, be (the) ruin (-ed, of), (be) overthrown, (cause to) stumble, X utterly, be weak. [Strong's]

Where and with who is it better to be humble? (Proverbs 16:19)

Who do we *not* want to divide the spoil with? (Proverbs 16:19)

___

Who will find good? (Proverbs 16:20)

___

What will you be if you trust in the Lord? (Proverbs 16:20)

___

Note: It is hard to trust in the Lord with a haughty and prideful spirit. This thing called humility is a choice and an act of your will.

What are we called to clothe/put on ourselves? (I Peter 5:5)

___

Where is this humility directed? (I Peter 5:5)

___

What is God opposed to? (I Peter 5:5; Proverbs 3:34)

___

Because God is opposed to the proud and gives grace to the humble, what should we do on our own without God having to do it for us? (I Peter 5:5)

___

Humility: tapeinophrosunē *(tap-i-nof-ros-oo'-nay) humiliation of mind*, that is, *modesty:* - humbleness of mind, humility (of mind), lowliness (of mind). [Strong's]

Humble [noun]: Tapeinos *(tap-i-nos')* Of uncertain derivation; *depressed*, that is, (figuratively) *humiliated* (in circumstances or disposition): - base, cast down, humble, of low degree (estate), lowly. [Strong's]

Humble yourselves [verb] tapeinoō *(tap-i-no'-o)* to *depress*; figuratively to *humiliate* (in condition or heart): - abase, bring low, humble (self). [Strong's]

Where should we be positioned when we humble ourselves? (I Peter 5:6)

What will be the cause and effect of us humbling ourselves under the mighty hand of God? (I Peter 5:6)

What are we able to do more effectively if we humble ourselves under the mighty hand of God? (I Peter 5:7)

How much of this anxiety should we cast on Him? (I Peter 5:7)

How does He feel about us and what we are anxious about? (I Peter 5:7)

Note: We started off talking about our plans, but when pride rises up we think we can accomplish our plans without God's direction. When we humble ourselves under God's hand of protection, we can cast our anxiety about our plans on Him and He will continue to direct us.

What is it that seems right unto a man? (Proverbs 16:25)

_____

What will be the end that seems right to a man? (Proverbs 16:25; 12:15; 14:12)

_____

Where is the lot cast? (Proverbs 16:33)

_____

Where is every decision from? (Proverbs 16:33)

_____

What are we called to do in the Lord? (Psalm 37:4)

_____

Delight: 'ânag *(aw-nag')* A primitive root; to be *soft* or pliable, that is, (figuratively) *effeminate* or luxurious: - delicate (-ness), (have) delight (self), sport self.

Note: This is more than just a jovial emotion, but more of a yielding to the Potter's hand, knowing that He is making you into something luxurious.

What is the cause and effect of delighting yourself in the Lord? (Psalm 37:4)

_____

Desire: mish'alah (*mish-aw-law'*) a *request:* - desire, petition. sha'al sha'el(*shaw-al', shaw-ale*) 'A primitive root; to *inquire*; by implication to *request*; by extension to *demand:* - ask (counsel, on), beg, borrow, lay to charge, consult, demand, desire, X earnestly, enquire, + greet, obtain leave, lend, pray, request, require, + salute, X straitly, X surely, wish. [Strong's]

Note: God will plan/give the desires and bring those desires to pass.

What must we do with the desires of our heart, our *way/plan*? (Psalm 37:5)

Commit: galal (*gaw-lal)'* A primitive root; to *roll* (literally or figuratively): - commit, remove, roll (away, down, together), run down, seek occasion, trust, wallow. [Strong's]

Trust: bâtach (*baw-takh'*) A primitive root; properly to *hie* for refuge; figuratively to *trust*, be *confident* or *sure:* - be bold (confident, secure, sure), careless (one, woman), put confidence, (make to) hope, (put, make to) trust. [Strong's]

What will happen when you commit your way and trust in the Lord? (Psalm 37:5

Pro-Verb Ponderings

We have plans, dreams, visions, hopes, goals; but without the Lord we have nothing. God has something for us also.

When we talk about our plans, what is really important is what God's plans are for us. While the Jews were in captivity in Babylon, God spoke forth His plans for them. (Check out Jeremiah 29 for full details.)

"For I know the *plans* that I have for you," declares the Lord. *Plans* for *welfare* and *not* for *calamity* to give you a *future* and a *hope.* Then you will call upon Me and *come* and *pray* to Me and *I will listen to you.* You will *seek* Me and *find* Me when you *search* for Me *with all your heart.*" (Jeremiah 29:11-13) [Emphasis mine]

This was written to a specific people at a specific time; however, it speaks of the heartbeat of God for His people, throughout the ages.

We continue tomorrow armed with the fact that God has good plans for us, but there will be strife as we will be tested. Be blessed in the testing.

PRO-VERBS 17

Proverbs 17:1, 3, 14, 19, 22, 27
The Strife Test

Strife is *not* a good thing. I hate to state the obvious, but people all over the world thrive - or would that be de-thrive - on this thing called strife. The book of Pro-Verbs shows the cause and effect of strife. Strife is a matter of the heart; and God can reveal by testing the heart and showing what rises to the top.

Strife: rîyb rib *(reeb, reeb)* a *contest* (personal or legal): - + adversary, cause, chiding, contend (-tion), controversy, multitude [from the margin], pleading, strife, strive (-ing), suit. {Strong's}

Test: bâchan *(baw-khan')* A primitive root; to *test* (especially metals); generally and figuratively to *investigate:* - examine, prove, tempt, try (trial). [Strong's]

What is the refining pot for? (Proverbs 17:3)

What is the furnace for? (Proverbs 17:3)

In contrast to pots and furnaces, and silver and gold, what does the Lord test? (Proverbs 17:3)

What is better than a house full of feasting with strife? (Proverbs 17:1)

> *Note: So begins the test; what type of house do you have? Remember, it is not the physical house, but the heart where the strife or peace flows.*

What is the beginning of strife like? (Proverb 17:14)

What should you do before the water of strife breaks out? (Proverbs 17:14)

Who loves strife? (Proverbs 17:19)

Who seeks destruction? (Proverbs 17:19)

> *Note: The door that is raised is the opening of the mouth, where strife flows out. The Pro-Verb - the Positive-Action - would be to keep the mouth shut.*

What is good medicine? (Proverbs 17:22)

What will dry up the bones? (Proverbs 17:22)

Pro-Verb Ponderings

Who has knowledge? (Proverbs 17:27)

___

Who has a cool spirit (human/ little "s")? (Proverbs 17:27)

___

What is a fool considered to be when he keeps silent? (Proverbs 17:28)

___

What is this fool considered to be when he closes his lips? (Proverbs 17:28)

___

Note: The test is what's in your heart; what is manifested on your lips; what is flowing out of your mouth. The Lord tests us for a purpose, and that purpose is for our good.

Pro-Verb Ponderings

*"But who can endure the day of His coming? And who can stand when He appears? For He is like a refiner's fire (purifies) and like fuller's soap (cleans). He will sit as a smelter and purifier of silver and he will purify the sons of Levi and refine them like gold and silver, so that they may present to the Lord offerings in righteousness. Then the offering of Judah and Jerusalem will be **pleasing to the Lord** as in the days of old and as in former years."*
Malachai 3:2-4 [emphasis mine]

Towers and tongues await us in tomorrow's ponderings. Get ready for your blessing today with expectancy for tomorrow.

PRO-VERBS 18

Proverbs 18:4, 6-8, 10-14, 18-21
Strong Towers and Powerful Tongues

Words are powerful; powerful to the point of life or death. Today, we will look at places of safety and how to avoid destruction.

What are the words of a man's mouth? (Proverbs 18:4)

___

What is the fountain of wisdom? (Proverbs 18:4)

___

What will a fool's lips bring? (Proverbs 18:6)

___

Note: No, we are not still in Proverbs 17. It is just that many similar themes intertwine throughout the Pro-Verbs.

What does the mouth of a fool call for? (Proverbs 18:6)

___

What is the ruin for a fool? (Proverbs 18:7)

___

What is a snare for the fool? (Proverbs 18:7)

What are the words of a whisperer like? (Proverbs 18:8)

Where do these dainty morsels (words of the whisperer) go down to? (Proverbs 18:8)

> Note: *These loose lips appear to be a danger that goes deep to the core of who we are, and begins to destroy us from the inside out. We need a safe place to go.*

What is the Name of the LORD? (Proverbs 18:10)

What happens if the righteous choose to run into the name of the Lord, a.k.a. *Strong Tower*? (Proverbs 18:10)

Name: shêm *(shame)* A primitive word (perhaps through the idea of definite and conspicuous *position*); an *appellation*, as a mark or memorial of individuality; by implication *honor, authority, character:* - + base, [in-] fame [-ous], name (-d), renown, report. [Strong's]

The LORD: yᵉhôvâh *(yeh-ho-vaw')* (the) *self Existent* or eternal; *Jehovah*, Jewish national name of God: - Jehovah, the Lord. hâyâh *(haw-yaw)'* A primitive root to *exist*, that is, *be* or *become, come to pass* (always emphatic and not a mere copula or auxiliary): - beacon, X altogether, be (-come, accomplished, committed, like), break, cause, come (to pass), continue, do, faint, fall, + follow, happen, X have, last, pertain, quit (one-) self, require, X use. [Strong's]

Note: There is one God with many names that describe His attributes. There are many compound names for God, including Jehovah Shalom (I AM your peace); Jehovah Raphe (I AM your healer); Jehovah Jireh (I AM your provider). On top of that, He is called El Shaddai (the breasty one with more than enough); Wonderful Counselor, Mighty God, Prince of Peace, Jesus (God is Salvation) Immanuel (God With Us).

Instead of speaking and living in strife, we have the promise of running into the Name Above All Names for safety and no strife.

Strong: 'ôz 'ôz (*oze, oze*) *strength* in various applications (*force, security, majesty, praise*): - boldness, loud, might, power, strength, strong. 'âzaz (*aw-zaz'*) A primitive root; to *be stout* (literally or figuratively): - harden, impudent, prevail, strengthen (self), be strong. [Strong's]

Tower: migdâl migdâlâh (*mig-dawl', mig-daw-law'*) a *tower* (from its size or height); by analogy a *rostrum*; figuratively a (pyramidal) *bed* of flowers: - castle, flower, pulpit, tower. [Strong's]

What is a rich man's wealth? (Proverbs 18:11)

What is this strong city's high wall like? (Proverbs 18:11)

What is the heart of a man before destruction? (Proverbs 18:12)

What goes before honor? (Proverbs 18:12)

> *Note: Man's strong cities can't hold a candle to the Lord's Strong Tower. You may build up around you, you may fortify with your imagination, but strife will tear it down from within.*

In what two ways does the Pro-Verbist describe when someone gives an answer before he hears? (Proverbs 18:13)

What can the spirit of a man (little 's') endure? (Proverbs 18:14)

What about the broken spirit? (Proverbs 18:14)

> *Note: Strife, words, pride, can break a spirit, if we allow it to. That is why we need to run into the Strong Tower and be safe.*

What puts an end to strife? (Proverbs 18:18)

What decides between mighty ones? (Proverbs 18:18)

What is harder to be won than a strong city? (Proverbs 18:19)

What are contentions like? (Proverbs 18:19)

Note: As definite as casting a lot is in putting an end to strife, offense and contentions can be built between mighty men stronger than the casting of lot. The mouth – words - can build walls, cities, strongholds.

What can satisfy a man? (Proverbs 18:20)

Fruit: pᵉrîy *(per-ee')* fruit (literally or figuratively): - bough, ([first-]) fruit ([-ful]), reward. pârâh *(paw-raw')* A primitive root; to *bear fruit* (literally or figuratively): - bear, bring forth (fruit), (be, cause to be, make) fruitful, grow, increase. [Strong's]

Note: Fruit is the end result, the product of something that started out with a seed that was planted, fertilized, cultivated, grown and harvested. The soil is the heart where the seed was planted. The fruit is the outworking that is manifested on the lips.

What state of being will a man be with the product of his lips? (Proverbs 18:20)

What is in the *power* of the *tongue*? (Proverbs 18:21)

What will those who love it do? (Proverbs 18:21)

Pro-Verb Ponderings

Satisfaction, dissatisfaction, death and life; all are linked to the mouth and the tongue. This is a running theme in the Pro-Verbs. The Pro-Verb Positive Action would be to begin planting *good seed* in the *soil/heart*. Water, fertilize and cultivate that seed with a renewed mind and a good confession, so when you are faced with strife, your *powerful tongue* will begin to speak forth *Life* instead of *Death*.

I love the positive-actions that we can utilize so that we will not live in the negative. Fools are often a theme in the Book of Pro-Verbs. Tomorrow we will see the way of the fool. I can't wait to see you tomorrow.

PRO-VERBS 19

Proverbs 19:1, 3-4, 7, 10, 13, 15, 17, 22, 24, 29
Poor Little Fool

In the 1950's, Ricky Nelson had a hit song called "Poor Little Fool." It was a catchy bit of rock and roll, but *fools* have been with us since Adam and Eve foolishly listened to the Serpent. In the Pro-Verbs, a fool and a poor person are often linked together, but that does not mean that someone who is poor is necessarily a fool, and poverty can be better than foolishness, depending on what the fool is doing.

What is it better for a poor man to be doing? (Proverbs 19:1)

Poor: rûsh *(roosh)* A primitive root; to *be destitute:* - lack, needy, (make self) poor (man). [Strong's]

Integrity: tôm *(tome) completeness*; figuratively *prosperity*; usually (morally) *innocence*: - full, integrity, perfect (-ion), simplicity, upright (-ly, -ness), at a venture. tâmam *(taw-mam')* A primitive root; to *complete* [Strong's]

Pro-Verb Ponderings

What is a poor man walking in integrity better than? (Proverbs 19:1)

What will ruin a man's way? (Proverbs 19:3)

What does the foolish man whose way is ruined (by his own foolishness) do towards God? (Proverbs 19:3)

Note: Like so many of us, we choose to rage before God and blame God for the problems that we caused. Psalm 14:1 states, "The fool has said in his heart, 'There is no God.'" What are you blaming on God that should be blamed on yourself or the devil?

What adds many friends? (Proverbs 19:4)

What is a poor man separated from? (Proverbs 19:4)

Note: It's sad but true; the vultures surround the wealthy - but they are really not true friends -while the poor are lonely, because nobody wants to be the friend of the poor.

What do the brothers of a poor man hate? (Proverbs 19:7)

Who abandons the poor man much more than his own family? (Proverbs 19:7)

___

Who does the poor man pursue with words? (Proverbs 19:7)

___

Where are those that the poor man pursues with his words? (Proverbs 19:7)

___

What is not fitting for a fool? (Proverbs 19:10)

___

What is not fitting for a slave? (Proverbs 19:10)

___

What is destruction to a father? (Proverbs 19:13)

___

What is like a constant dripping? (Proverbs 19:13)

___

What casts someone into a deep sleep? (Proverbs 19:15)

___

What will an idle man suffer? (Proverbs 19:15)

___

Pro-Verb Ponderings

Who lends to the Lord (as if He needs it)? (Proverbs 19:17)

___

What will the Lord do to the lender? (Proverbs 19:17)

___

What is desirable in a man? (Proverbs 19:22)

___

What is it better to be, rather than being a liar? (Proverbs 19:22)

___

What does the sluggard bury his hand in? (Proverbs 19:22)

___

Sluggard: 'âtsêl *(aw-tsale) indolent:* - slothful, sluggard. 'âtsal *(aw-tsal')* A primitive root; to *lean* idly, that is, to be *indolent* or *slack:* - be slothful. [Strong's]

When the sluggard's hand is buried in the dish, what is the sluggard too lazy to do? (Proverbs 19:24)

___

What is prepared for scoffers? (Proverbs 19:29)

___

What is for the back of fools? (Proverbs 19:29)

___

Pro-Verb Ponderings

Fools don't just happen; they are created by daily choices. Being poor is just a lack of funds, but a fool is someone who has a lack of wisdom. What is really foolish is having wisdom readily available to you, yet choosing to not avail yourself of that wisdom.

Day 20 is on its way. Be wise and get ready. See ya tomorrow.

PRO-VERBS 20

Proverbs 20:5, 9, 17-20, 24, 27
The Lamplighter

Plans, dreams, goals and desires are common to man, but we need guidance from the Lord. The guidance system is found within us; it is called the human spirit. For us to be able to carry out our plans, we must draw from the depths of our souls, hear the voice of God and then do what we hear. Faith without works is dead; and so will our plans be.

Where is the plan of man located? (Proverbs 20:5)

___

What is this plan like? (Proverbs 20:5)

___

What will a man of understanding do to this plan in the deep water? (Proverbs 20:5)

___

> *Note: If the plan is not drawn out, it is only a wish. It is only something that someone has dreamed, but never did anything about.*

Who can say they have cleansed their own heart? (Proverbs 20:9)

Who can say, "I am pure from my sin?" (Proverbs 20:9)

---

*Note: The implied answer is a resounding, **'Nobody.'** "As it is written, "There is none righteous, no not one." (Romans 3:10) "For all have sinned and fall short of the glory of God." (Romans 3:23) "Therefore, just as through one man sin entered into the world, and death through sin, and so death spread to all men, because all sinned." (Romans 5:12) "For the love of Christ controls us, having concluded this that one died for all, therefore all died and He died for all, so that they who live might no longer live for themselves but for Him who died and rose again on their behalf." (II Corinthians 5:14-15) "All of us like sheep have gone astray, each of us has turned to his own way; but the Lord has caused the iniquity of us all to fall on Him." (Isaiah 53:6)*

What is bread obtained by falsehood? (Proverbs 20:17)

What will it be afterwards in his mouth? (Proverbs 20:17)

How should we prepare plans? (Proverbs 20:18)

Pro-Verb Ponderings

How should we make war? (Proverbs 20:18)

What does a slanderer reveal? (Proverbs 20:19)

Who should we not associate with? (Proverbs 20:19)

Note: The key to wartime strategy is Top Secret. We don't want the enemy to know our plans because the enemy could counter our intelligence. The devil is our enemy. He has schemes and plans for us, and they ain't good. The Word says that there is safety in a multitude of counselors but everyone in a multitude may not be a good counselor; they could be a slanderer who will reveal our plans.

What has the Lord done to a man's steps? (Proverbs 20:24)

Can man understand his way? (Proverbs 20:24)

What is the spirit of man? (Proverbs 20:27)

What is the lamp of the Lord searching? (Proverbs 20:27)

Pro-Verb Ponderings

The only thing worse than stumbling around in total darkness, is to have a little bit of light and falling flat on your face. I was once walking down some steps in a dimly lighted garage, missed the bottom step and slammed my face into a block wall in a matter of seconds. Thank you Lord for lighting our way.

I cannot wait to see you tomorrow as we look at how the word *"but"* can be used in the positive or in the negative. See ya tomorrow - no ifs, ands or…

Pro-Verb Ponderings

PRO-VERBS 21

Proverbs 21:1-5, 8, 11, 15, 20, 28, 31
The 'But' Factor

Things in our lives appear to be set, to be floating along - not subject to change - until we look into *The 'But' Factor*. The word *'but'* is a word of contrast. "*But* the Lord…" "*But* everyone…" "*But* as for the pure…" "*But* when the wise…" "…*But* is terror to the wicked." "*But* a foolish man..." "*But* the man who listens…" "*But* victory belongs to the Lord…" are all examples of The 'But' Factor in our latest Pro-Verb. This Pro-Verb shows the cause and effect of various attitudes and concepts.

What is the king's heart like? (Proverbs 21:1)

Heart: leb *(labe)* the *heart*; also used (figuratively) very widely for the feelings, the will and even the intellect; likewise for the *centre* of anything [Strong's]

Channels/River: Peleg *(peh'-leg)* a *rill* (that is, small *channel* of water, as in irrigation): - river, stream. [Strong's]

Where are these heart channels located? (Proverbs 21:1)

Hand: yâd *(yawd)* A primitive word; a *hand* (the *open* one (indicating *power, means, direction*) [Strong's]

Where does the Lord turn the heart of the king? (Proverbs 21:1)

Wishes/Will: châphêts (*khaw-fates'*) A primitive root; properly to *incline* to; by implication (literally but rarely) to *bend*; figuratively to *be pleased* with, *desire:* - X any at all, (have, take) delight, desire, favour, like, move, be (well) pleased, have pleasure, will, would. [Strong's]

What is right in every man's own eyes? (Proverbs 21:2)

[*'But' Alert*]

What does the Lord weigh? (Proverbs 21:2)

What is desired by the Lord for you to do as opposed to sacrifice? (Proverbs 21:3)

What produces sin? (Proverbs 21:4)

What surely leads to an advantage? (Proverbs 21:5)

[*'But' Alert*]

What will surely result in poverty? (Proverbs 21:5)

Pro-Verb Ponderings

What is the way of a guilty man? (Proverbs 21:8)

___

['But' Alert]

How is the conduct of the pure? (Proverbs 21:8)

___

Who becomes wise when the scoffer is punished? (Proverbs 21:11)

___

['But' Alert]

What does the wise receive when he is instructed? (Proverbs 21:11)

___

What is joy for the righteous? (Proverbs 21:15)

___

['But' Alert]

What is the exercise of justice to the workers of iniquity? (Proverbs 21:15)

___

What two things are in the dwellings of the wise? (Proverbs 21:20)

___

[*'But' Alert*]

What does a foolish man do with the precious treasure? (Proverbs 21:20)

___

What will be the end result for a false witness? (Proverbs 21:28)

___

[*'But' Alert*]

What will the man who listens to truth do? (Proverbs 21:28)

___

What does a wicked man display? (Proverbs 21:29)

___

[*'But' Alert*]

What does the upright do? (Proverbs 21:29)

___

What three things are *not* against the Lord? (Proverbs 21:30)

___
___
___

Pro-Verb Ponderings

What is prepared for the day of battle? (Proverbs 21:31)

Prepared: kûn *(koon)* A primitive root; properly to *be erect* (that is, stand perpendicular); hence (causatively) to *set up*, in a great variety of applications, whether literal *(establish, fix, prepare, apply)*, or figurative *(appoint, render sure, proper* or *prosperous)* [Strong's]

[*'But' Alert*]

What does belong to the Lord? (Proverbs 21:31)

Victory/Safety: tᵉshuʻâh tᵉshuʻâh *(tesh-oo-aw', tesh-oo-aw'):* rescue (literally or figuratively, personal, national or spiritual): - deliverance, help, safety, salvation, victory. shâvaʻ *(shaw-vah')* A primitive root; properly to *be free*; but used only causatively and reflexively to *halloo* (for help, that is, *freedom* from some trouble): - cry (aloud, out), shout. [Strong's]

Pro-Verb Ponderings

The contrast between the wise and the foolish is very eye opening to me. Maybe if we weigh our actions by contrasting the cause and effect before we do something, we would avoid negative effect to our cause.

Are we having fun yet? God's wisdom is an amazing thing. When your world gets negative, then factor in the positive and live a wise life in a foolish world. See you tomorrow for more of the positive same.

PRO-VERBS 22

Proverbs 22:22-29
The 'Do Not' Counsel

I hesitate focusing on the *Do Not* verses, because there are so many *Do* verses in the Word. In a world where people view Christianity's rules and regulations as nothing but *do and don't rules*, we want to put our best foot forward. But ya can't just ignore the *Do Not* verses. Keep your eyes on the C&E Principle (Cause and Effect). Proverbs 22:17-21 is the Pro-Verbist giving out wise words. We are called to incline our ears, hear the words of the wise, have these pleasant words on our lips so our trust may be in the Lord. The Pro-Verbist taught and wrote these excellent words of counsel and knowledge and made known the *certainty* of the *words of truth* so that we may *correctly answer* Him who sent us. Now; The *Do Not* Counsel.

Who should we not rob because he is poor? (Proverbs 22:22)

Poor: dal *(dal)* properly *dangling*, that is, (by implication) *weak* or *thin:* - lean, needy, poor (man), weaker. dálal *(daw-lal')* A primitive root; to *slacken* or *be feeble*; figuratively to *be oppressed:* - bring low, dry up, be emptied, be not equal, fail, be impoverished, be made thin. [Strong's]

Who should we not crush at the gate? (Proverbs 22:22)

Afflicted: ʿânîy *(aw-nee')* *depressed*, in mind or circumstances - afflicted, humble`, lowly`, needy, poor. [Strong's]

Who will plead their case? (Proverbs 22:23)

What will be the ultimate cause and effect of robbing the poor and crushing the afflicted? (Proverbs 22:23)

Who should you not associate with? (Proverbs 22:24)

Who should you not go with? (Proverbs 22:24)

Why should you not associate with a man of anger or go with a hot tempered man? (Proverbs 22:25)

Associate/Friendship: râʿâh *(raw-aw')* A primitive root; to *tend* a flock, that is, *pasture* it; intransitively to *graze* (literally or figuratively); generally to *rule*; by extension to *associate* with (as a friend): - X break, companion, keep company with, devour, eat up, evil entreat, feed, use as a friend, make friendship with, herdsman, keep [sheep] (-er), pastor, + shearing house, shepherd, wander, waste. [Strong's]

Pro-Verb Ponderings

Anger: 'aph (*af*); properly the *nose* or *nostril*; hence the *face* and occasionally a *person*; also (from the rapid breathing in passion) *ire:* - anger (-gry), + before, countenance, face, + forbearing, forehead, + [long-] suffering, nose, nostril, snout, X worthy, wrath. ânaph (*aw-naf'*) A primitive root; to *breathe* hard, that is, *be enraged:* - be angry (displeased). [Strong's]

Hot-tempered/Furious: chêmâh chêmâ' (*khay-maw', khay-maw'*); *heat*; figuratively *anger, poison* (from its *fever*): - anger, bottles, hot displeasure, furious (-ly, -ry), heat, indignation, poison, rage, wrath (-ful). yâcham (*yaw-kham'*) A primitive root; Probably to *be hot*; figuratively to *conceive:* - get heat, be hot, conceive, be warm. [Strong's]

What will happen to you *if* you do learn the ways of the hot-tempered man and the man given to anger? (Proverbs 22:25)

Who should you not be among? (Proverbs 22:26)

Who else beside the giver of pledges should you not be among? (Proverbs 22:26)

What could happen *if* you can't pay debts for which you have agreed to be guarantor, or given your pledge to? (Proverbs 22:27)

What should you *not* move? (Proverbs 22:28)

Who set these ancient boundaries? (Proverbs 22:28)

Who will stand before kings? (Proverbs 22:29)

Who will the man who is skilled in his work *not* stand before? (Proverbs 22:29)

Pro-Verb Ponderings

Do not consent is wisdom to every enticement. This is the perfect Pro-Verb companion to Pro-Verbs 1:10.

Tomorrow, we see this applying to our appetites. Sometimes we just have to say 'no' to our desires. See ya tomorrow.

PRO-VERBS 23

Proverbs 23:1-3, 6-8, 20-21, 29-35
Appetite Control

The old saying is, "eat, drink and be merry, for tomorrow you may die." The quote is found in various locations in the Bible, including Ecclesiastes 8:15, Isaiah 22:13 and I Corinthians 10:31. Here in our latest Pro-Verb, we have some advice on what we eat and why we need to control our appetites.

What should you carefully consider when you sit down to dine with a ruler? (Proverbs 23:1)

What should you put to your throat? (Proverbs 23:2)

What is the deciding factor about putting a knife to your throat? (Proverbs 23:2)

> *Note: When you sit down with a ruler, there may be other reasons and motives for him eating with you. He may want to poison you. Putting a knife to your throat is a precautionary, symbolic restraint method. It is also wise from a diet perspective.*

> *Note: Great appetites are linked to our flesh nature. We eat too much amd we drink too much when we have no control or discipline in our lives.*

What should we not desire? (Proverbs 23:3)

_____

What type of food is the ruler's food considered to be? (Proverbs 23:3)

_____

What should you not eat from the selfish man? (Proverbs 23:6)

_____

What should you not desire from the selfish man? (Proverbs 23:6)

_____

What is the selfish man like within himself? (Proverbs 23:7)

_____

What will the selfish man tell you, or encourage you to do? (Proverbs 23:7)

_____

As the selfish man encourages you to eat and drink, what is not with you? (Proverbs 23:7)

_____

Note: Temptation - and the tempter - does not have your best interest at heart. They desire to pull you away from who you are and cause you harm.

What will you do with the morsel you have eaten? (Proverbs 23:8)

_____

What will you have wasted (*Oh, how good this tastes*) once you have vomited up the morsel you have eaten? (Proverbs 23:8)

_____

Who should you not be with? (Proverbs 23:20)

_____

What will be the end result of the heavy drinker and the glutton? (Proverbs 23:21)

_____

What will the heavy drinker and glutton be clothed with? (Proverbs 23:21)

_____

Note: "Hang around dogs and ya get fleas." (Unknown) The company you keep will bring you down if you hang around long enough and do the things they do. I know that Jesus hung out with sinners - and was accused of being a glutton and a winebibber - but at the same time there is a danger in having close associations with sinners. Instead of them becoming like the Christ in you, you become like the devil in them.

Pro-Verb Ponderings

Note: Proverbs 23:29 asked the "who questions." Proverbs 29:30-35 answers the "who questions." Who has (1) woe, (2) contentions, (3) complaining, (4) wounds without cause, (5) redness of eyes?

What do they linger over? (Proverbs 23:30)

___

What do they taste? (Proverbs 23:30)

___

What should you not look on? (Proverbs 23:31)

___

What should the red wine not be doing? (Proverbs 23:31)

___

How does that wine go down? (Proverbs 23:31)

___

What are the two after-effects once that smooth wine goes down? (Proverbs 23:32)

___

Note: In today's world, drinking is just being sociable. There is a plethora of drinks with many clever names that call out to us. Some of those drinks are smooth, enjoyable; but in the end, Kaboom! It bites and stings like a poisonous viper/serpent. In Christianity, we are free to drink; but so many times that freedom turns into an opportunity for the flesh, and before you know it you are trapped.

What will your *eyes* see? (Proverbs 23:33)

What will your *mind* utter? (Proverbs 23:33)

Note: When you don't restrain what you eat and drink, there is cause and effect. The principle applies to thoughts and actions: unrestrained thoughts produce unrestrained words, resulting in unrestrained actions. When the Pro-Verbist says your mind will, "utter perverse things" he speaks of our thought life speaking to our souls, that will eventually come out of our physical mouths and eventually manifest in our actions. There is nothing worse than a drunk speaking and doing things.

What will you be like? (Proverbs 23:34)

Note: Drowned and hanging over a precipitous place are what you will be like. It will be like a sailor who is, "three sheets into the wind."

What happens when someone strikes you while you are drunk? (Proverbs 23:35)

What is your awareness level when they beat you? (Proverbs 23:35)

Pro-Verb Ponderings

Note: When you get so drunk that you don't know what is happening to you, you are too drunk.

What will you do when you awake from the drunken stupor? (Proverbs 23:35)

Pro-Verb Ponderings

Sometimes we tend to eat just because there is food before us. When our provider is on the scene, we do not have to worry about not having food for tomorrow. We don't have to gorge ourselves into a stupor. I like what Paul writes about immorality and food, "Food is for the stomach and the stomach is for food; but God will do away with both of them. Yet the body is not for immorality, but for the Lord and the Lord is for the body." (I Corinthians 6:13)

Tomorrow we are hitting the 24 mile-marker on our Pro-Verb journey. Are you prepared? If not, tomorrow is for you. Be blessed.

PRO-VERBS 24

Proverbs 24:2-5, 8-10, 27, 30-34
The Art of Preparation

In this dog-eat-dog world, successful people plan for success. There appears to be two types of people: those who are driven to success, and those who feed off of other people's success. In a world of Type A personalities, I am on the other end of the spectrum as a Type Z personality. The type A personality tends to be such a *nitpicker* of details that they can take all of the fun out of whatever they are planning, thus ruining it for all of us Type Z people who tend to leave the *nits unpicked* because they like to be surprised along the journey of life.

Some people are so laid back that they enter into the realm of being a sluggard. Pro-Verbs - and the book of James - speak of being prepared so you will not enter into poverty.

> *Note: I know that this is about the book of Pro-Verbs, but James lays out the heart and attitude that we should have about goal planning and preparation to accomplish things - not only in business - but in life.*

What time frame do some put on making a profit? (James 4:13)

Where will they go to make this profit? (James 4:13)

___

How long will they stay in "such and such a city" to make that profit? (James 4:13)

___

What will they engage in? (James 4:13)

___

What do we not know? (James 4:14)

___

What are we like? (James 4:14)

___

What is the nature of vapor? (James 4:14)

___

What is the end result of vapor? (James 4:14)

___

What should you say instead of stating that you will go into "such and such a city," spend a year there, engage in business and make a profit? (James 4:15)

___

When we don't submit our goals to the Lord what are we boasting in? (James 4:16)

___

Pro-Verb Ponderings

What is this boasting considered to be? (James 4:16)

If you know the right thing to do - about submitting to God's will - and don't do it, what is that considered to be? (James 4:17)

How is a house built? (Proverbs 24:3)

How will a house be established? (Proverbs 24:3)

How will the rooms of that 'Wisdom House' be filled? (Proverbs 24:4)

With what type of riches will this house be filled? (Proverbs 24:4)

What will one that plans to do evil be called by men? (Proverbs 24:8)

What is the devising of folly considered to be? (Proverbs 24:9)

Note: Remember James 4:17 - Therefore, to one who knows the right thing to do and does not do it, to him it is sin.

What is the scoffer considered to be by men? (Proverbs 24:9)

___

What is the cause and effect if you are slack in the day of distress? (Proverbs 24:10)

___

Where should you prepare your work? (Proverbs 24:27)

___

Where should your work be made ready for yourself? (Proverbs 24:27)

___

What should you do after your preparation and readiness? (Proverbs 24:27)

___

Whose field did the Pro-Verbist pass by? (Proverbs 24:30)

___

Whose vineyard did the Pro-Verbist pass by? (Proverbs 24:30)

___

Pro-Verb Ponderings

What was this field and vineyard completely overgrown with? (Proverbs 24:31)

_____

What was the condition of the stone wall? (Proverbs 24:31)

_____

As the Pro-Verbist reflected upon what he saw, what did he receive? (Proverbs 24:32)

_____

What will bring on poverty? (Proverbs 24:33)

_____

How will your poverty come upon you? (Proverbs 24:34)

_____

What will your want (need, scarcity, penury, beggary) come like? (Proverbs 24:34)

_____

Rodney Boyd

Pro-Verb Ponderings

We started out with James, showing that planning alone is not enough. Planning *plus* submitting plans to the will of God results in success. Not submitting your plans to the Lord results in sin and folly. However, we see in Pro-Verbs - the book of Positive-Action - that planning will bring success; and not planning ends in folly and destruction. So, wake up from your sleep; wake up from your slumber; unfold your hands. Get to work and plan to avoid the robber and want (need, scarcity, penury, beggary) in your life.

Tomorrow let's get a dross reading in our lives. Caution, fire is required. See ya tomorrow.

PRO-VERBS 25

Proverbs 25:4-5, 11-13, 28
Silver Minus Dross=VESSEL

As the song goes, *"Lord, you are more precious than silver. Lord, you are more costly than gold. Lord, you are more beautiful than diamonds and nothing I desire compares with you."* God started humanity with a lump of clay, filled with the breath of God. When the fall came, the living lump of clay became a vessel of dishonor. Jesus came with the Death, Burial and Resurrection, and became the propitiation/substitute for our sins. He cleansed us with the His own blood, and we became lumps of clay with the glory of God manifested in us. As we walk out our faith until the return of God, we are being changed into His image, as the manifested dross is removed. Let's check out the Pro-Verb Process.

What needs to be taken away? (Proverbs 25:4)

_____

Dross: sîyg sûg *(seeg, soog)* in the sense of *refuse; scoria:* - dross. [Strong's]

From where is the dross taken away? (Proverbs 25:4)

_____

Silver: keseph (*keh'-sef*) *silver* (from its *pale* color); by implication *money:* - money, price, silver (-ling). [Strong's]

What is the outcome of the removal of dross from the silver? (Proverbs 25:4)

Vessel: k^{e}lîy (*kel-ee'*) something *prepared*, that is, any *apparatus* (as an implement, utensil, dress, vessel or weapon): - armour ([-bearer]), artillery, bag, carriage, + furnish, furniture, instrument, jewel, that is made of, X one from another, that which pertaineth, pot, + psaltery, sack, stuff, thing, tool, vessel, ware, weapon, + whatsoever. [Strong's]

Honer/For the Finer: tsâraph (*tsaw-raf'*) A primitive root; to *fuse* (metal), that is, *refine* (literally or figuratively): - cast, (re-) fine (-er), founder, goldsmith, melt, pure, purge away, try. [Strong's]

> *Note: II Timothy speaks of all kinds of vessels in a large house. There are vessels of gold, silver, wood, earthenware; some to honor and some to dishonor. Paul speaks of the vessel cleansing himself and becoming a vessel of honor - sanctified (set aside for a purpose) - and useful to the Master, prepared for every good work. Of course, only the Lord can ultimately cleanse us, but we become part of the process as we (1) flee from youthful lusts; (2) pursue righteousness - including faith, love and peace - along with others who call on the Lord from a pure heart. Part of the cleansing process is to refuse foolish and ignorant speculations, knowing that they produce quarrels. (II Timothy 2:20-23)*

Who is the de-drossed vessel for? (Proverbs 25:4)

What is - should be - taken away from the king? (Proverbs 25:5)

What is the cause and effect of the wicked (dross) being taken away from before the king (God)? (Proverbs 25:5)

What will the throne (vessel) be established in? (Proverbs 25:5)

Throne: kisse' kisseh (*kis-say'*, *kis-say'*) properly *covered*, that is, a *throne* (as *canopied*): - seat, stool, throne. kâsâh (*kaw-saw'*) A primitive root; properly to *plump*, that is, *fill up* hollows; by implication to *cover* (for clothing or secrecy): - clad self, close, clothe, conceal, cover (self), (flee to) hide, overwhelm. [Strong's]

Established: kûn (*koon*) A primitive root; properly to *be erect* (that is, stand perpendicular); hence (causatively) to *set up*, in a great variety of applications, whether literal (*establish, fix, prepare, apply*), or figurative (*appoint, render sure, proper* or *prosperous*): - certain (-ty), confirm, direct, faithfulness, fashion, fasten, firm, be fitted, be fixed, frame, be meet, ordain, order, perfect, (make) preparation, prepare (self), provide, make provision, (be, make) ready, right, set (aright, fast, forth), be stable, (e-) stablish, stand, tarry, X very deed. [Strong's]

Righteousness: Tsedeq (*tseh'-dek*) the *right* (natural, moral or legal); also (abstractly) *equity* or (figuratively) *prosperity:* - X even, (X that which is altogether) just (-ice), ([un-]) right (-eous) (cause, -ly, -ness). [Strong's]

What kind of apples does the Pro-Verbist refer to? (Proverbs 25:11)

Where are these golden apples set? (Proverbs 25:11)

The apples of gold in settings of silver are like what? (Proverbs 25:11)

When are these gold and silver words spoken? (Proverbs 25:11)

Note: In Ephesians 4:29, we see that we are not to allow unwholesome words to proceed from our mouths. Verse 31 defines those unwholesome words as words of bitterness, wrath, anger, clamor and slander. We see in verse 30 that these words grieve the Holy Spirit. What we are to allow to proceed from our mouths are words of edification - building up words, words that are tender-hearted, forgiving, like God in Christ has done for us. The time frame for allowing these words to proceed from our mouths is the need of the moment. When we allow these words to proceed, they give grace. The receivers of this grace are those who hear.

Pro-Verb Ponderings

These words are what the Pro-Verbist says are, a word spoken in the right circumstance.

What type of earring is spoken of? (Proverbs 25:12)

What type of ornament? (Proverbs 25:12)

Who is like the earring and ornament of gold? (Proverbs 25:12)

Reprover: yakach *(yaw-kakh')* A primitive root; to *be right* (that is, correct); reciprocally to *argue*; causatively to *decide, justify* or *convict:* - appoint, argue, chasten, convince, correct (-ion), daysman, dispute, judge, maintain, plead, reason (together), rebuke, reprove (-r), surely, in any wise. [Strong's]

Who is the one who wisely reproves speaking to? (Proverbs 25:12)

Listening/Obedient: shâma' *(shaw-mah')* A primitive root; to *hear* intelligently (often with implication of attention, obedience, etc.; causatively to *tell*, etc.): - X attentively, call (gather) together, X carefully, X certainly, consent, consider, be content, declare, X diligently, discern, give ear, (cause to, let, make to) hear (-ken, tell), X indeed, listen, make (a) noise, (be) obedient, obey, perceive, (make a) proclaim (-ation), publish, regard, report, shew (forth), (make a) sound, X surely, tell, understand, whosoever [heareth], witness. [Strong's]

Pro-Verb Ponderings

Many years ago, there was a group called the Hollywood Argyles with a hit record called "Alley Oop." The man behind the group and song was Gary S. Paxton, who went on to be a prolific Contemporary Christian Artist with a strange look and a wry sense of humor. Gary S. Paxton ("Don't forget the "S." It's one-third of my whole name.") wrote and sang about the Vessel of Honor. "A vessel of honor of God, a vessel of honor for God, sanctified, holy, so we might be a vessel of honor for God." (*A Vessel of Honor for God* by Gary S. Paxton)

What makes us the vessel of honor is not what is on the outside, but *Who* is on the inside. As Bruce Coble, my mentor and the Missions Pastor of Springhouse Worship and Arts Center, says, "We are lumps of clay filled with the glory of God."

Tomorrow we check out fools, sluggards and gossips. Check it out and make sure you are not in that group (I know you are not). Be blessed on your journey.

PRO-VERBS 26

Proverbs 26 (various verses) Of Fools, Sluggards and Gossips

Usually, we put in the verses that we will be covering in the chapter. This time, however, there are so many to choose from, I elected to just go through and pick out various verses. The categories of choices include *fools*, *sluggards* and *gossips*.

FOOLS

Fool: kᵉsîyl (*kes-eel'*) properly *fat*, that is, (figuratively) stupid or *silly:* - fool (-ish). kâsal (*kaw-sal'*) A primitive root; properly to *be fat*, that is, (figuratively) *silly:* - be foolish. [Strong's]

What is not fitting for a fool? (Proverbs 26:1)

_____

What happens if you answer a fool? (Proverbs 26:4)

_____

How should we answer a fool? (Proverbs 26:5)

_____

What will the fool not be wise in *if* you answer him has he deserves? (Proverbs 26:5)

_____

Pro-Verb Ponderings

Note: Verse 5 is not a contradiction of verse 4. In these two verses, we are told not to answer a fool, but they do not say to not answer the fool at all. Don't answer him according to his folly; but do answer a fool as his folly deserves.

What kind of animal is a fool like? (Proverbs 26:11)

___

What does this dog return to? (Proverbs 26:11)

___

What does this vomit represent? (Proverbs 26:11)

___

Note: This is the verse that Peter quotes in II Peter 2:22 when he speaks of false teachers.

SLUGGARDS

Slothful/Sluggard/Lazy: 'âtsêl *(aw-tsale) indolent:* - slothful, sluggard. 'âtsal *(aw-tsal')* A primitive root; to *lean* idly, that is, to be *indolent* or *slack:* - be slothful. [Strong's]

In what two places does the sluggard/lazy man claim there are lions? (Proverbs 26:13)

___

What analogy is used to describe how a sluggard is attached to his bed? (Proverbs 26:14)

___

Where does the sluggard bury his hand? (Proverbs 26:15)

What is the sluggard too weary to do once his hand is in the dish? (Proverbs 26:15)

In whose eyes is the sluggard wise? (Proverbs 26:16)

When compared, to whom does the sluggard consider himself wiser than? (Proverbs 26:16)

> *Note: The bottom line is, the sluggard is lazy. When there is danger of lions or violence in the street, all he can do is identify the problem. He is so lazy - like a door turns on its hinges – that he cannot get out of bed. His hand gets to the dish, but he is too lazy to feed himself. His wisdom in his own eyes is more than seven men who can give a discreet answer, compared to foolish answers.*

GOSSIPS

Whisperer/Gossip: nirgân (*neer-gawn'*) From an unused root meaning to *roll* to pieces; a *slanderer:* - talebearer, whisperer. [Strong's]

What does a meddler do with dogs' ears, or what is he like? (Proverbs 26:17)

Pro-Verb Ponderings

What does the meddler *meddle* with when he passes by? (Proverbs 26:17)

Do the things the meddler *meddles with* belong to him? (Proverbs 26:17)

What does the madman throw? (Proverbs 26:18)

Who does the madman deceive? (Proverbs 26:19)

When the madman deceives his neighbor, what does he say? (Proverbs 26:19)

Note: Once the words of fire, piercing and death leave the mouth, saying that you were just joking to the wounded and dead does not mean anything. The damage is done. So it is with gossips and slanderers.

When there is no more wood what happens to the fire? (Proverbs 26:20)

What happens when the whisperers and gossipers stop whispering and gossiping? (Proverbs 26:20)

What are charcoal (to hot embers) and wood (to fire) like compared to the contentious man? (Proverbs 26:21)

___

What does the one who *hates* disguise his lips with? (Proverbs 26:24)

___

Pro-Verb Ponderings

Fools, Sluggards and Gossips. Are you one? What fires are you fueling with your lips? Are you a lover or a hater? Be a Wise man/woman, a productive person and have lips of love.

We are approaching out final destination with five more stops along the way. Stop Number 27 is just up ahead. See you tomorrow.

Rodney Boyd

PRO-VERBS 27

Proverbs 27:5-6, 9-10, 14, 17
Friendly Fire

Christian recording artist Michael W. Smith extols the virtues of a friend when he sings, *"Friends are friends forever…"* but he qualifies that statement by adding, *"if the Lord's the Lord of them."* A true friend is not someone who just strokes your ego; but someone who will tell you the truth, especially when you are going astray down the wrong road.

Friend: rêaʻ rêyaʻ (*ray'-ah, ray'-ah*) an *associate* (more or less close): - brother, companion, fellow, friend, husband, lover, neighbour, X (an-) other. raʻah (*raw-aw'*) A primitive root; to *tend* a flock, that is, *pasture* it; intransitively to *graze* (literally or figuratively); generally to *rule*; by extension to *associate* with (as a friend): - X break, companion, keep company with, devour, eat up, evil entreat, feed, use as a friend, make friendship with, herdsman, keep [sheep] (-er), pastor, + shearing house, shepherd, wander, waste. [Strong's]

What is better than love that is concealed? (Proverbs 27:5)

Rebuke: okêchah tokachath (*to-kay-khaw', to-kakh'-ath*) *chastisement*; figuratively (by words) *correction, refutation, proof* (even in defence): - argument, X chastened, correction, reasoning, rebuke, reproof, X be (often) reproved. yâkach *(yaw-kakh')* A primitive root; to *be right* (that is, correct); reciprocally to *argue*; causatively to *decide, justify* or *convict:* - appoint, argue, chasten, convince, correct (-ion), daysman, dispute, judge, maintain, plead, reason (together), rebuke, reprove (-r), surely, in any wise. [Strong's]

Is the rebuke concealed? (Proverbs 27:5)

What is the rebuke better than? (Proverbs 27:5)

Note: The rebuke is upfront, not behind your back. That would be gossip and backstabbing; but a true friend loves you enough to confront you.

What makes the heart glad? (Proverbs 27:9)

What is the counsel of man to his friend? (Proverbs 27:9)

Counsel: 'êtsâh *(ay-tsaw')*; *advice*; by implication *plan*; also *prudence:* - advice, advisement, counsel ([-lor]), purpose. yâ'ats *(yaw-ats')* A primitive root; to *advise*; reflexively to *deliberate* or *resolve:* - advertise, take advice, advise (well), consult, (give take) counsel (-lor), determine, devise, guide, purpose. [Strong's]

Who should you *not* forsake? (Proverbs 27:10)

Whose house should you *not* go to? (Proverbs 27:10)

When should you *not* go to your brother's house? (Proverbs 27:10)

Who is better than a brother far away? (Proverbs 27:10)

> *Note: This is not saying a brother relationship is not a good thing. It is saying that when family is far away, a good neighbor – a friend - is a good thing in the day of calamity.*

What will cause a blessing to be considered a curse? (Proverbs 27:14)

Should a man bless his friend quietly or loudly? Does the time of day that a man blesses his friend matter? (Proverbs 27:14)

> *Note: At first this one – blessing turned into a curse - puzzled me. It looks like it is not a good thing to bless a friend, but it dawned on me: an early morning blessing. The people who don't like your loud blessing, will try to turn this good thing into a bad thing. So, keep on blessing loudly.*

Pro-Verb Ponderings

What sharpens iron? (Proverbs 27:17)

In comparison to iron sharpening iron, what sharpens a man? (Proverbs 27:17)

Sharpens: châdad *(khaw-dad')* A primitive root; to *be* (causatively *make*) *sharp* or (figuratively) *severe:* - be fierce, sharpen. [Strong's]

> *Note: Metal on metal; metal on flint; man to man. This speaks of one on one; bringing a piece of metal to a finely honed edge that is sharper and more productive in its cutting edge. So it is with friends - brothers in the Lord - who will sharpen each other. Sometimes, in the sharpening process there may be some sparks.*

Who will eat the fruit of a fig tree? (Proverbs 27:18)

Who will be honored? (Proverbs 27:18)

What is reflected in water? (Proverbs 27:19)

What does the heart of man reflect? (Proverbs 27:19)

> *Note: If a man is sharpened by another man - as we tend to do for each other - the reflection of the heart should be of a sharpened man.*

Bonus Note: This has nothing to do with the friend theme or maybe it does. I just found it funny.

What is the constant dripping on a day of steady rain like? (Proverbs 27:15)

Contentious: midyân (*mid-yawn'*) brawling, contention (-ous). mâdôn (*maw-dohn'*) a *contest* or quarrel: - brawling, contention (-ous), discord, strife. [Strong's]

What is it like when you try to restrain the contentious woman? (Proverbs 27:16)

Pro-Verb Ponderings

In the world of social media, people accept people as their friends, just to see how many friends they can accumulate. You may have 1,000 friends on your social network, but in reality, you might be able to count your real friends on one hand.

Tomorrow we delve into true wealth. We will need true wisdom and positive actions to handle that wealth. Be blessed tomorrow as you become wealthy beyond money.

PRO-VERBS 28

Proverbs 28:4-5, 7, 11, 13, 19-22, 25-27
The Law of Wealth

Proverbs 28 continues with the thought started in Proverbs 27; *Pro-Verbs concerning actions*. The sub-heading in my Bible breaks down the various actions with the words, "in relation to." It begins with 'in relation to *Life*,' transitions in chapter 28 to 'in relation to *Law*,' and 'in relation to *Wealth*,' and will go into chapter 29 with 'in relation to *Stubbornness*.' It is how the *Pro-Verbs Positive Action* is intertwined within our lives.

What do those who forsake the law do? (Proverbs 28:4)

_____

What do those who keep the law do with them? (Proverbs 28:4)

_____

What do evil men *not* understand? (Proverbs 28:5)

_____

Who understands all things? (Proverbs 28:5)

_____

Pro-Verb Ponderings

Who is a discerning son? (Proverbs 28:7)

Who humiliates his father? (Proverbs 28:7)

Note: To forsake or to keep the law - that is the question. Of course, as believers in Jesus the Christ we know that Jesus did not come to destroy the law, but to fulfill it. We know that, as we walk in grace - the law was a teacher - but grace frees us from rules, regulations, etc. The Word of God - the laws or principles of the Kingdom - is what we focus on now. We are still called to keep His law and the greatest is, "to love the Lord with all our heart, soul, mind and strength," and the second greatest law to keep is, "to love our neighbors as ourselves." (Matthew 22:37; Mark 12:30; Luke 10:27) Jesus said, "He who has My commandments and keeps them, he it is who loves me. He who loves me will be loved by My Father and I will love him and will manifest/disclose/reveal myself to him. (John 14:21)

What shall not depart from your mouth? (Joshua 1:8)

Meditate: hâgâh *(haw-gaw)'* A primitive root to *murmur* (in pleasure or anger); by implication to *ponder:* - imagine, meditate, mourn, mutter, roar, X sore, speak, study, talk, utter. [Stong's]

NOTE: To ruminate (mooin' and chewin') on the Word of God.

What will you meditate on? What is the *It* that you will meditate on? (Joshua 1:8)

What is the time frame of this meditation? (Joshua 1:8)

What will you be careful to do, according to Joshua 1:8?

Written in what? (Joshua 1:8)

What will you then make? (Joshua 1:8)

Prosperous: tsâlach tsâlêach *(tsaw-lakh', tsaw-lay'-akh)* A primitive root; to *push* forward, in various senses (literally or figuratively, transitively or intransitively): - break out, come (mightily), go over, be good, be meet, be profitable, (cause to, effect, make to, send) prosper (-ity, -ous, -ously). [Strong's]

What will you then have? (Joshua 1:8)

What kind of success will it be? (Joshua 1:8)

Good Success: sâkal *(saw-kal')* A primitive root; to *be* (causatively *make* or *act*) *circumspect* and hence *intelligent*: -

consider, expert, instruct, prosper, (deal) prudent (-ly), (give) skill (-ful), have good success, teach, (have, make to) understand (-ing), wisdom, (be, behave self, consider, make) wise (-ly), guide wittingly. [Strong's]

Note: Prosperity is enough to meet your needs and an overflow to help meet the needs of others, and Good Success is the ability to accomplish what God has purposed in your life. This is all hinged on your relationship to the Law (the Word of God) and your R.R.M. (Renewed Meditating Mind).

In whose eyes is the rich man wise? (Proverbs 28:11)

Who sees through the rich man who is wise in his own eyes? (Proverbs 28:11)

Who will *not* prosper? (Proverbs 28:13)

Who will find compassion? (Proverbs 28:13)

Who will have plenty of good food? (Proverbs 28:19)

Who will have poverty? (Proverbs 28:19)

How much poverty will they have? (Proverbs 28:19)

___

Who will abound with blessings? (Proverbs 28:20)

___

What happens to him who makes haste to be rich? (Proverbs 28:20)

___

What is *not* good? (Proverbs 28:21)

___

Why is showing partiality *not* good? (Proverbs 28:21)

___

What will a man do for a piece of bread? (Proverbs 28:21)

___

Who hastens after wealth? (Proverbs 28:22)

___

What does the evil-eyed, wealth-hastener *not* know? (Proverbs 28:22)

___

Who stirs up strife? (Proverbs 28:25)

___

Pro-Verb Ponderings

In contrast to the arrogant man who stirs up strife, who will the Lord prosper? (Proverbs 28:25)

_____

What is someone who *trusts in his own heart* instead of the Lord? (Proverbs 28:26)

_____

What will be the outcome of someone who walks wisely (trusting the Lord)? (Proverbs 28:26)

_____

What will be the *want factor* of those who give to the poor? (Proverbs 28:27)

_____

Who will have many curses? (Proverbs 28:27)

_____

Who is he shutting his eyes to? (Proverbs 28:27)

_____

Pro-Verb Ponderings

The apostle Paul writes to Timothy, his son in the faith, about this thing called money. "The love of money is the root of all sorts of evil, and some longing for it have wandered away from the faith, and pierced themselves with many a pang." (I Timothy 6:10) The Pro-Verbist gets to the *root* of the problem that affects not only lust for wealth but affects our spiritual lives as well.

Jesus would say something and then tell them that if they had ears, they should *hear* what He was saying. He was implying that they needed to hear physically with their ears, but more than that, listen and perceive what He was saying. Tomorrow, Jesus would want those who have eyes to see, be visionary and perceive within and not just what you see. Hmmm…sounds like a faith thing to me. Be blessed with 20/20 vision tomorrow.

PRO-VERBS 29

Proverbs 29:1, 11, 16, 18, 22-23, 25
The Visionary

As someone who has worn glasses since the first grade, I appreciate vision. The ability to see clearly and not just blurred images is a good thing. Sometimes I tend to see things spiritually in blurred, out of focus vision. Thank God for corrective spiritual surgery restoring me back to 20/20 vision.

What happens when there is *no vision*? (Proverbs 29:18)

Vision: châzôn *(khaw-zone')* a *sight* (mentally), that is, a *dream, revelation*, or *oracle:* - vision. châzâh *(khaw-zaw)* A primitive root; to *gaze* at; mentally to *perceive, contemplate* (with pleasure); specifically to *have a vision of:* - behold, look, prophesy, provide, see. [Strong's]

Perish: pâra' *(paw-rah')* A primitive root; to *loosen*; by implication to *expose, dismiss*; figuratively *absolve, begin:* - avenge, avoid, bare, go back, let, (make) naked, set at naught, perish, refuse, uncover. [Strong's]

> Note: *"Without a vision the people are unrestrained/perish." (NASB). If you don't have a vision, you are loosened/not reigned in/out of control/unrestrained.*

Who will be happy? (Proverbs 29:18)

Note: The Law keeps people restrained. So it is with the Word of God in our lives. When you have insight – vision of what the Word of God says - and do what it says, you will be restrained/not do wrong and be happy. For example, if the Word says (and it does say), "do not commit adultery," and you are unrestrained and commit adultery, you will not be happy.

Ruminator Saying: "Unrestrained thoughts (what we think) results in unrestrained words (what we say about what we think), resulting in unrestrained actions (what we do about what we say and think). Restraint starts with the renewed mind renewed by the washing of the water of the Word of God. That is where our vision comes from.

What happens to a man who hardens his neck *after much reproof*? (Proverbs 29:1)

Reproof: tôkêchâh tôkachath *(to-kay-khaw', to-kakh'-ath) chastisement*; figuratively (by words) *correction, refutation, proof* (even in defence): - argument, X chastened, correction, reasoning, rebuke, reproof, X be (often) reproved. yâkach *(yaw-kakh')* A primitive root; to *be right* (that is, correct); reciprocally to *argue*; causatively to *decide, justify* or *convict*: - appoint, argue, chasten, convince, correct (-ion), daysman, dispute, judge, maintain, plead, reason (together), rebuke, reprove (-r), surely, in any wise. [Strong's]

Pro-Verb Ponderings

How quickly will this happen? (Proverbs 29:1)

How badly will this neck be broken? (Proverbs 29:1)

Who always looses his temper? (Proverbs 29:11)

What will a wise man do instead of losing his temper? (Proverbs 29:11)

What is the cause and effect of when the wicked increases? (Proverbs 29:16)

Wicked: râshâ˓ (*raw-shaw'*) morally *wrong*; concretely an (actively) *bad* person: - + condemned, guilty, ungodly, wicked (man), that did wrong. râshâ˒ (*raw-shah'*) A primitive root; to *be* (causatively *do* or *declare*) *wrong*; by implication to *disturb, violate:* - condemn, make trouble, vex, be (commit, deal, depart, do) wicked (-ly, -ness). [Strong's]

Increases: râbâh (*raw-baw'*) A primitive root; to *increase* (in whatever respect): - [bring in] abundance (X -antly), + archer, be in authority, bring up, X continue, enlarge, excel, exceeding (-ly), be full of, (be, make) great (-er, -ly), X -ness), grow up, heap, increase, be long, (be, give, have, make, use) many (a time), (any, be, give, give the, have) more (in number), (ask, be, be so, gather, over, take, yield) much (greater, more), (make to) multiply, nourish, plenty (-eous), X process [of time], sore, store, thoroughly, very. [Strong's]

Transgression: pesha' *(peh'-shah)* a *revolt* (national, moral or religious): - rebellion, sin, transgression, trespassive pâsha' *(paw-shah')* A primitive root; to *break* away (from just authority), that is, *trespass, apostatize, quarrel:* - offend, rebel, revolt, transgress (-ion, -or).

Who stirs up strife? (Proverbs 29:22)

_____

Who abounds in transgression? (Proverbs 29:22)

_____

What will bring a man low? (Proverbs 29:23)

_____

What will a humble spirit obtain? (Proverbs 29:23)

_____

What are we to clothe ourselves with? (I Peter 5:5)

_____

What is the direction of this clothed humility? (I Peter 5:5)

_____

Who is God opposed to? (I Peter 5:5/Proverbs 3:34)

_____

Who does God give grace to? (I Peter 5:5/Proverbs 3:34)

Pro-Verb Ponderings

Because God opposes the proud and gives grace to the humble, what should we do? (I Peter 5:6)

Who does the exaltation? (I Peter 5:6)

Who does the humbling? (I Peter 5:6)

What is your self-humbling down under? (I Peter 5:6)

When will you be exalted *after* your self-humbling? (I Peter 5:6)

Under this humbled exaltation, what are we to cast on Him? (Proverbs 5:7)

> *Note: When you are too proud, you think you can handle your own problems, and all you meet is resistance from God. However, when you humble yourself, you will turn to God, because He cares for you. It is only when you are humble, that you can resist the roaring devil lion and avoid being devoured.*

What brings a snare? (Proverbs 29:25)

What will happen to the one who humbly trusts the Lord? (Proverbs 29:25)

Pro-Verb Ponderings

It is time to get a humble vision and walk upright in the Lord. In 1972, Johnny Nash had a song entitled, "I Can See Clearly Now." In the midst of a negative, blurred world he speaks of seeing clearly. God's desire is for us to see clearly. Vision is very important in how you view and perceive things in your life.

GODISNOWHERE. If you look at this sentence, you may see GOD IS **NO WHERE**, or if you took a second look you may see it differently as, GOD IS **NOW HERE**. It all depends on how you look at it. Adjust your vision and see God in everything. It will change your life.

The journey in the Land of Pro-Verbs is almost over, but there is so much to see. Be blessed and keep your eyes wide open so you won't miss out on anything.

Rodney Boyd

PRO-VERBS 30

Proverbs 30:24-28; 32-33
Small Things

The old saying is, "Good things come in small packages." That is true, but the opposite is also true; "Bad things come in small packages." There are so many topics to choose from in Proverbs 30; wisdom oozes out of these pages. Proverbs 30:32-33 may be my favorite Pro-Verb - but I do have a lot of favorites.

How many things are found on planet earth which are *small* but exceedingly wise? (Proverbs 30:24)

Ant: nᵉmâlâh *(nem-aw-law')* an *ant* (probably from its almost *bisected* form): - ant. [Strong's]

Shephanim/Conie: shâphân *(shaw-fawn')* a species of *rock rabbit* (from its *hiding*), that is, probably the *hyrax:* - coney. sâphan *(saw-fan')* A primitive root; to *conceal* (as a valuable): - treasure. [Strong's]

Locust: arbeh *(ar-beh)'* a *locust* (from its rapid *increase*): - grasshopper, locust. [Strong's]

Lizard/Spider: sᵉmâmîyth *(sem-aw-meeth')* in the sense of *poisoning*; a *lizard* (from the superstition of its *noxiousness*): - spider. shâmêm *(shaw-mame')* A primitive root; to *stun* (or intransitively *grow numb*), that is, *devastate* or (figuratively) *stupefy* (both usually in a passive sense): - make amazed, be astonished, (be an) astonish (-ment), (be, bring into, unto, lay, lie, make) desolate (-ion, places), be destitute, destroy (self), (lay, lie, make) waste, wonder. [Strong's]

What are ants *not*? (Proverbs 30:25)

What do these "not strong people" – a.k.a. ants - do in the summer? (Proverbs 30:25)

What are the shephanim (conies/rock rabbit) *not*? (Proverbs 30:26)

Where do the non-mighty shephanim (conies/rock rabbit) make their houses? (Proverbs 30:26)

What do the locusts *not* have? (Proverbs 30:27)

How do the non-king locust go out? (Proverbs 30:27)

How can you grasp the lizard/spider? (Proverbs 30:28)

Where is this small creature that you can grasp with your hand found? (Proverbs 30:28)

Note: These four things are small, especially in the eyes of man, but they do mighty things. These mighty things are positive attributes that we can draw on as human beings. We can learn the art of preparation (consecration) from the ant. We can live within the rock (Jesus); walk in divine unseen order (obedience) and live in the presence of the Lord (king's palace). The Word says, "Let the weak say he is strong," and by faith we, "call things that are not as though they were." I find great Kingdom Concepts in these small examples of wisdom from the Pro-Verbs.

Note: Now we come to one of my favorite Pro-Verbs; Proverbs 30:32-33, that speaks of a small thing that is also a powerful thing for the negative. This Pro-Verb gives wisdom on how to deal with self-exaltation and plotting of evil, and also shows the principle of Cause and Effect.

What have you been foolish in doing? (Proverbs 30:32)

Exaltation: nâsâ' nâsâh (*naw-saw', naw-saw'*): (A primitive root; to *lift*, in a great variety of applications, literally and figuratively, absolutely and relatively: - accept, advance, arise, (able to, [armour], suffer to) bear (-er, up), bring (forth), burn, carry (away), cast, contain, desire, ease, exact, exalt (self), extol, fetch, forgive, furnish, further, give, go on, help, high, hold up, honourable (+ man), lade, lay, lift (self) up, lofty, marry, magnify, X needs, obtain, pardon, raise (up), receive, regard, respect, set (up), spare, stir up, + swear, take (away, up), X utterly, wear, yield. [Strong's]

What have you been plotting? (Proverbs 30:32)

Plotting: zâmam (*zaw-mam'*) A primitive root; to *plan*, usually in a bad sense: - consider, devise, imagine, plot, purpose, think (evil). [Strong's]

What is the Number One principle *if* you have been foolishly exalting your self and have been plotting evil? (Proverbs 30:32)

Note: What is exalted and plotted, of course, starts from within. The number one way of preventing plotted exaltation from become reality, is by placing your hand over your mouth, because that is where the small thing lies. The tongue is small but powerful.

What happens if you put a bit into a horse's mouth? (James 3:3)

Bridle: chalinagōgeō (*khal-in-ag-ogue-eh'-o*) to *be* a *bit leader*, that is, to *curb* (figuratively): - bridle. [Strong's]

Bit: Chalinos (*khal-ee-nos'*) a *curb* or *head stall* (as *curbing* the spirit): - bit, bridle. [Strong's]

What do we direct by placing a bit in the horse's mouth? (James 3:3)

Rodney Boyd

What are the great ships? (James 3:4)

What are these great ships driven by? (James 3:4)

What are these great, wind-driven ships directed by? (James 3:4)

Rudder: pēdalion *(pay-dal'-ee-on)* Neuter of a (presumed) derivative of πηδόν pēdon - the *blade* of an oar; a "pedal," that is, *helm:* - rudder. [Strong's]

Who is in control of the very small rudder that directs the ship? (James 3:4)

Where is the ship directed? (James 3:4)

In contrast to the horse and the ship - that is directed at the pleasure of the rider and the pilot - what is a *small part* of the body? (James 3:5)

Tongue: glōssa *(gloce'-sah)* Of uncertain affinity; the *tongue*; by implication a *language* (specifically one naturally unacquired): - tongue. [Strong's]

Note: This small thing called the tongue is located in the mouth where self-exaltation takes place and where evil is

> *plotted. How we speak - and what we speak - determines where we go and how we manifest obedience to the Lord. To control the tongue, place your hand over your mouth.*

In comparison to the *large body*, what is the tongue? (James 3:5)

Even though the tongue is small, what does the tongue boast about? (James 3:5)

What is the great forest set on fire/aflame by? (James 3:5)

What is the tongue? (James 3:6)

What is the tongue the very world of? (James 3:6)

Iniquity: adikia *(ad-ee-kee'-ah)* (legal) *injustice* (properly the quality, by implication the act); moral *wrongfulness* (of character, life or act): - iniquity, unjust, unrighteousness, wrong. adikos *(ad'-ee-kos) unjust*; by extension *wicked*; by implication *treacherous*; specifically *heathen:* - unjust, unrighteous. [Strong's]

What is the tongue set among? (James 3:6)

What does the tongue defile? (James 3:6)

Defile: spiloō *spee-lo'-o*; to *stain* or *soil* (literally or figuratively): - defile, spot. spilos (*spee'-los*) a *stain* or *blemish*, that is, (figuratively) *defect, disgrace:* - spot. [Strong's]

How much of the body does the tongue defile? (James 3:6)

What does the tongue set on fire? (James 3:6)

Course: trochos (*trokh-os'*) a *wheel* (as a *runner*), that is, (figuratively) a *circuit* of physical effects: - course. trechō (*trekh'-o*) Apparently a primary verb (properly θρέχω threchō; compare which uses δρέμω dremō, *drem'-o* as an alternate in certain tenses; to *run* or *walk hastily* (literally or figuratively): - have course, run. [Strong's]

What is the course of our life set on fire by? (James 3:6)

Fire: phlogizō (*flog-id'-zo*) to *cause a blaze*, that is, *ignite* (figuratively to *inflame* with passion): - set on fire. phlox (*flox*) (to "flash" or "flame"); a *blaze:* - flame (-ing). [Strong's]

Hell: Geenna (*gheh'-en-nah*) Of Hebrew origin; *valley of* (the son of) *Hinnom*; *gehenna* (or *Ge-Hinnom*), a valley of Jerusalem, used (figuratively) as a name for the place (or state) of everlasting punishment: - hell. [Strong's]

> *Note: The Valley of Hinnom (Gehenna) was a garbage dump - a place for discarded refuse - outside the walls of Jerusalem that burned 24 hours a day. Hell is when you are outside the gates of the presence of God, and burn for 24 hours a day. That is the root of self-exaltation and the plotting of evil.*

What has been *tamed* by the human race? Every species of what has been tamed? (James 3:7)

Tamed: damazō (*dam-ad'-zo*) A variation of an obsolete primary of the same meaning; to *tame:* - tame. [Strong's]

Who can tame the tongue? (James 3:8)

What kind of evil is the tongue? (James 3:8)

What is the tongue full of? (James 3:8)

What two things do we do with this same mouth? (James 3:9)

Who is it that we curse? (James 3:9)

Who have these men that we curse with our mouth *been made in the likeness of*? (James 3:9)

What comes out of the same mouth? (James 3:10)

Should things be this way, *the same mouth with blessings and curses*? (James 3:10)

What does a fountain *not* send out from the same opening? (James 3:11)

Sweet Water: glukus (*gloo-koos'*) Of uncertain affinity; *sweet* (that is, not bitter nor salt): - sweet, fresh. [Strong's]

Bitter Water: Pikros (*pik-ros'*) (through the idea of *piercing*); *sharp* (*pungent*), that is, *acrid* (literally or figuratively): - bitter. [Strong's]

What can a fig tree *not* produce? (James 3:12)

What can a vine *not* produce? (James 3:12)

What can salt water not produce? (James 3:12)

Fresh Water: glukus *(gloo-koos')* *sweet* (that is, not bitter nor salt): - sweet, fresh. [Strong's]

Note: In John 4 Jesus speaks of a well that is placed within us. This well is our human spirit. Jesus says that we can draw from this well, and that out of this well - found in our innermost being - will flow rivers of living water. He was talking about the Holy Spirit. Within us - in the core of who we are - is our spirit; our innermost being. We are told that out of our hearts flows the issues of life. If that inner place is polluted by sin, what flows out is what is inside of you. If you shake a cup of coffee and coffee comes out, the question is asked, "Why did coffee come out of that shaken cup?" Most will answer, "Because it was shaken." But the real answer is, coffee came out of that cup because that is what was in the cup. The shaking only revealed what is in there. So it is with our words. When we are shaken by world events, personal tragedy, etc., what comes out of our mouth reveals our heart.

Only God can change a man's heart - but we can control what comes out of the mouth. Remember our Ruminator saying, "Unrestrained thoughts (what we think) produces unrestrained words (what we say), resulting in unrestrained actions (what we do)." Now back to the self-exalting, evil plotting mouth.

What does the churning of milk produce? (Proverbs 30:33)

Churning: mîyts *(meets) pressure:* - churning, forcing, wringing. mûts *(moots)* A primitive root; to *press,* that is, (figuratively) to *oppress:* - extortioner. [Strong's]

Produces/Brings Forth: yâtsâ' *(yaw-tsaw')* A primitive root; to *go* (causatively *bring*) *out* [Strong's]

What does the pressing of the nose bring forth? (Proverbs 30:33)

Note: Churning and pressing speaks of actions that produce something. Cream being churned produces butter, and taking a nose and pressing/wringing brings forth (produces) blood. Now the comparison.

What does the churning/agitation of anger produce? (Proverbs 30:33)

Note: The mouth/heart is the churn. The tongue is the agitator. The constant speaking out of anger is the agitation. Just like cream/milk is put in a butter churn, and the agitator begins to do it's job by agitating what is in the churn, producing butter, so it is with what is within our mouth/heart. As we begin to speak out of anger, the churning begins, and the end result is strife. The key to this Pro-Verb is to place the hand over the mouth, to regulate the churning if there is evil and plotting in the churn/heart/mouth.

Pro-Verb Ponderings

This principle works for the negative - and produces negative – but, it also works for the positive - producing positive. The first step is to *renew the mind with the Word of God*. Place that in your heart - and your mouth - and then begin to *churn with your tongue* (confession/saying the same word as God says about a situation) and the end result - or what is produced - will be the will of God. Elvis Presley had a song in the 70's called *Burning Love*. I always think of that song when I read this Pro-Verb. If we place *Love* in the churn/mouth/heart, and we begin to churn/agitate/speak *Love*, we will have what is known from the Elvis song, *"A hunk-a-hunk of churning Love/Churning Love."* Mix in *God Stuff*, and start *churning*.

Here we are, 30 days into our journey and we are now approaching our final day. I would say that I have saved the best for last, but how can I say that when every day was the best. It is like the head of the wedding marveling at the wine that Jesus changed from water:

> *"...every man serves the good wine first, and when men have drunk freely, then that which is poorer; you have kept the good wine until now."*
>
> John 2:10

Well, let us continue in the *now* and check out the wife of all wives, The Pro-Verbs 31 Wife.

PRO-VERBS 31

Proverbs 31:10-31
The Proverbs 31 Wife

Well, here we are in the last chapter of the Book of Pro-Verbs. Of course, it is not the last chapter of us walking in Positive-Action. It is only the beginning. If you have hung in there to this point, you are a true Ruminator. Remember, we only gleaned from the Pro-Verbs. There are a lot more nuggets that you can read and re-read, and still never exhaust the wisdom of *Pro-Verbs Positive Action*. Let's take a look at the Proverbs 31 Wife and use her example *not* just of an excellent wife, but as the template or example of the Bride of Christ for all of us, regardless of our gender.

> *Note: Many times a woman will read this section and lament that they are not like the Proverbs 31 Wife, so why even try. Well, this is the standard, much like Christ and His righteousness is our standard. We can only obtain by being in Him and not trusting our own righteousness or goodness. So it is with this standard; we strive for the standard and allow God to form in us this most excellent of women (also applies to men).*

What is the description of this wife? (Proverbs 31:10)

Pro-Verb Ponderings

What is her worth above? (Proverbs 31:10)

What does the heart of her husband do? (Proverbs 31:11)

What will her husband have no lack of? (Proverbs 31:11)

What does she do for him? (Proverbs 31:12)

What does she *not* do for him? (Proverbs 31:12)

How long will she do him good? (Proverbs 31:12)

What does she look for? (Proverbs 31:13)

Once she finds the wool and flax, what does she do in delight? (Proverbs 31:13)

What is she like? (Proverbs 30:14)

What does she bring from afar? (Proverbs 30:14)

When does she rise? (Proverbs 30:15)

___

Who does she give food to? (Proverbs 30:15)

___

Who does she give portions of food to? (Proverbs 30:15)

___

What does she consider? (Proverbs 30:16)

___

What does she do with her consideration? (Proverbs 30:16)

___

What does she pay for her consideration with? (Proverbs 30:16)

___

What does she gird herself with? (Proverbs 30:17)

___

As she girds herself with strength, what does she make her arms? (Proverbs 31:17)

___

What does she sense? (Proverbs 31:18)

___

Pro-Verb Ponderings

What does not go out at night? (Proverbs 31:18)

_____

What does she reach out her hands to? (Proverbs 31:19)

_____

Note: The distaff is a staff for holding wool, which is twisted into thread and wound on the spindle.

What do her hands grasp? (Proverbs 31:19)

_____

Who does she extend her hands to? (Proverbs 31:20)

_____

Who does she stretch out her hands to? (Proverbs 31:20)

_____

What three things does she extend and stretch her hands out to? (Proverbs 31:19-20)

_____

_____

_____

What is she not afraid of for her household? (Proverbs 31:21)

_____

Why is she not afraid of the snow? (Proverbs 31:21)

_____

Who does she make coverings for? (Proverbs 31:22)

___

What's her clothing made out of? (Proverbs 31:22)

___

Where is her husband known? (Proverbs 31:23)

___

Who does her husband sit among? (Proverbs 31:23)

___

What does she do with the linen garments she makes? (Proverbs 31:24)

___

Who does she supply belts to? (Proverbs 31:24)

___

Compared to the clothing that she makes for herself, what is her clothing? (Proverbs 31:25)

___

What does our Proverbs 31 Wife smile at? (Proverbs 31:25)

___

What does she open her mouth in? (Proverbs 31:26)

___

What is on her tongue? (Proverbs 31:26)

How does she look to the ways of her household? (Proverbs 31:27)

What kind of bread does she not eat? (Proverbs 31:27)

What do her children do when they rise up? (Proverbs 31:28)

What does her husband also do when He rises up? (Proverbs 31:28)

Who has done nobly? (Proverbs 31:29)

Compared to the many daughters who have done nobly, how has the Proverbs 31 Wife done? (Proverbs 31:29)

What is charm? (Proverbs 31:30)

Deceitful: sheqer *(sheh'-ker)* an *untruth*; by implication a *sham* (often adverbially): - without a cause, deceit (-ful), false (-hood, -ly), feignedly, liar, + lie, lying, vain (thing), wrongfully. [Strong's]

What is beauty? (Proverbs 31:30)

Vain: hebel hăbêl (*heh'-bel, hab-ale'*) *emptiness* or *vanity*; figuratively something *transitory* and *unsatisfactory*; often used as an adverb: - X altogether, vain, vanity. [Strong's]

In comparison to deceitful charm and vain beauty, what shall the woman who fears the Lord be? (Proverbs 31:30)

What should you give to her? (Proverbs 31:31)

What should you let her works be? (Proverbs 31:31)

Where should her works be praised? (Proverbs 31:31)

Pro-Verb Ponderings

Pro-Verbs *begins* with *fearing the Lord* and *ends* with *fearing the Lord*. It begins with *the beginning of knowledge* and ends with *being praised for fearing the Lord*. Sometimes wives may wonder how they could possibly live up to the standard of the Pro-Verbs 31 Woman. Probably the same way the Christians in general can live up to what a Christian should be like, by faith with the help of the Helper, the Holy Spirit.

For those who have been faithful and finished this devotional/workbook, you are *true Ruminators*, who *Moo* and *Chew* on the *Cud of the Word of God*. Moo to you!

Normally, at this place we would add a blessing for the next day's reading. The good news is that we only gave you a thumbnail sketch of all the good wisdom in the book of Pro-Verbs. You can go back at the beginning of each month, and glean from the book of Positive Action and write your own devotional.

It has been an honor to be your traveling companion with you on this journey.

Also Available From
WordCrafts Press

Never Run A Dead Kata
by Rodney Boyd Ni Dan

Morning Mist
(Stories from the water's edge)
by Barbie Loflin

Why I Failed in the Music Business
(and how NOT to follow in my footsteps)
by Steve Grossman

Youth Ministry is Easy!
(and 9 other lies)
by Aaron Shaver

Chronicles of a Believer
by Don McCain

Illuminations
by Paula K. Parker & Tracy Sugg

www.wordcrafts.net

www.ingramcontent.com/pod-product-compliance
Lightning Source LLC
Chambersburg PA
CBHW031416290426
44110CB00011B/399